Distance Education in Social Work

Planning, Teaching, and Learning

Distance does make a difference

Warmest regards

Paul Abels

Paul Abels is Professor Emeritus at California State University, Long Beach where he also served as Director of the Social Work Program. He received his doctorate in Social Administration from the University of Chicago, and taught for 21 years at the School of Applied Social Science at Case Western Reserve University in Cleveland.

Dr. Abels was a Fulbright Scholar in Turkey and Iran and with his wife Sonia Leib Abels helped start a school of social work in Lithuania. He has been both a practitioner and administrator in social agencies working with groups and individuals; a community organizer in public housing; and the director of a Vista Training Program in Cleveland. He is currently the President of the Association for the Advancement of Social Work With Groups.

Distance Education in Social Work

Planning, Teaching, and Learning

Paul Abels, PhD, MSW, Editor

 Springer Publishing Company

Springer Publishing Company, Inc.
11 West 42nd Street
New York, NY 10036-8002

Acquisition Editor: Shoshana Bauminger
Production Editor: Janice Stangel
Cover Design by Joanne Honigman

05 06 07 08 09/5 4 3 2 1

Library of Congress Cataloging-in-Publication Data

Distance education in social work : planning, teaching, and learning / Paul Abels, editor.
    p. cm.
  Includes bibliographical references and index.
  ISBN 0-8261-2475-5
  1. Social work education.   2. Distance education.   I. Abels, Paul, 1928–

  HV11.D596 2005
  361.3'071'1—dc22   2004026376

Printed in the United States of America by Integrated Book Technology

To S.L.A. and all the others who helped me learn
how to change my mind

CONTENTS

CONTRIBUTORS

Paul Abels, MSW, PhD. Professor Emeritus, Department of Social Work, California State University, Long Beach

Kathleen Crew, MSW. Site Coordinator, Distance Education Program for CSULB at California State University, Hayward

Agathi Glezakos, MSW, PhD, Department of Social Work Private Practice. Faculty Member, California State University, Long Beach

James J. Kelly, MSW, PhD. Associate Vice President for Extended and Continuing Education, California State University, Hayward

Christine B. Kleinpeter, MSW, Psy.D. Professor, Department of Social Work, California State University, Long Beach

Marilyn K. Potts, MSW, PhD. Professor, Department of Social Work, California State University, Long Beach

Frank B. Raymond III, MSW, PhD. Distinguished Dean/Professor Emeritus. Coordinator, International Programs, College of Social Work, University of South Carolina, Columbia

Jo Ann R. Coe Regan, MSW, PhD. Professor. Distance Education Coordinator. California State University, Long Beach

PREFACE

James J. Kelly, MSW, PhD

My interest in distance education began in Hawaii. Hawaii is a likely spot for thoughts about using technology to communicate across vast spaces. A series of once isolated islands in the middle of the Pacific Ocean, Hawaii is a place where communication with the outside world has been a key issue in development. I like to think that I was one of the people who helped Hawaii to overcome its educational isolation, and that I applied what I learned to the task of using technology to connect and help people all over the world

A SHORT STORY ABOUT DISTANCE EDUCATION AND TECHNOLOGY

When I moved to Hawaii in 1975, the islands were isolated from the rest of the world in ways that would be hard to imagine today. For example, we received national television news reports at 6:00 a.m. the next morning. These reports were those broadcast on the mainland the previous day! Other television programming was even more delayed—by a week or longer. And library patrons ordering journal issues could expect to receive them 3 to 6 months later than their colleagues in California and New York.

This is what it was like as a new graduate from Brandeis University, when I took my first faculty job at the University of Hawaii. Each summer during my graduate studies, I returned to the University of Southern California Andrus Gerontology Center in Los Angeles to take seminars in my specialty: gerontology. I was able to learn from internationally renowned leaders in the field of aging and wondered how I might bring this sort of educational experience in aging to Hawaii. There were three experts in aging at the University in Oahu. But most of the aging population, and the social workers who served them lived on the outer islands. There was little contact between the university and the outer islands. Determined to overcome this barrier, I began my first foray into distance education. In those days, distance education meant that educators were sent onto the traveling circuit for face-to-face classroom instruction and interaction with students. The program was a great success. For the first time, social workers on the islands were able to benefit from training on their home turf. But travel limited outreach. (The only way to get from island to island was by air or sea.) Enter serendipity. I learned that the university had a long-standing contract with NASA to make use of a satellite communication system no longer needed by the space agency. It was called PEACES AT. For the first time, we were able to broadcast faculty lectures from the main island to the outlying islands in the South Pacific. The broadcasts—which were audio- but not video-interactive—helped extend the reach of our program.

A few years later I found myself teaching gerontology in Long Beach, California. I believed that I would be coming to a place that was rich in social work resources and free of the isolation of an island state. What I found was a bit different California produced relatively few graduate-trained social workers. (At that time, the city of New York produced more MSW graduates each year than did the entire state of California.) The geographical expanse of the state meant that many small towns and rural counties had no access to professional training in social work.

As a faculty member, and later director, of the Department of Social Work, I set about to do in California what I had done successfully in Hawaii. Traditionally, social workers who wanted to earn an MSW degree and lived in rural areas had to leave their home communities for the 2-year educational program. The program with the cooperation of many faculty and staff successfully continues to grow.

Technology, as illustrated by programs such as distance education, is changing the structure and nature of educational institutions in our society. Its effect upon social work education, the social welfare institutions, and the consequences are important areas for us to examine as we become involved in those changes. In this book a myriad of authors experienced in DE programs describe, explain, analyze, and present the issues, problems, and challenges they encounter in their DE experience. The lessons gleaned from all experiences in DE are valuable for faculties, schools, and students in social work.

It is a general belief that the usual connections among and between faculty and students have been restructured somewhat in DE programs. There is little doubt that DE compensates and contributes to the society by expanding opportunities for more persons to become professional social workers. More social work professionals are entering the field as a result of the expansion of social work education through DE; and it appears that it is one of the solutions for expanding educational opportunities in social work education.

Distance education makes possible the crossing and unlocking of borders, economic as well as geographical, not only from one part of a country to another, but from one nation to another. It establishes a community of national cohorts where everyone can learn from each other and from well-respected and recognized scholars in the profession who teach the knowledge needed for their degrees in social work.

As do members of other professions, I believe social workers can aid society in achieving social justice for more persons. We make the assumption that increased educational opportunities can promote these goals.

This book, written by faculty involved in teaching, administrating, and assessing DE programs in social work, offers readers perspectives on the issues, problems, strengths, design, and methods of DE. The book shows the patterns, variety, and potential of DE programs as well as the thinking and doing needed in developing and maintaining a quality program. Its efforts to show the inner workings of distance education programs makes it a valuable contribution to the literature on social work education.

Dr. Kelly is Associate Vice President for Extended and Continuing Education, California State University, Hayward

ACKNOWLEDGMENTS

I appreciatively thank the many persons who contributed to the development of this book. First, the students whose ideas and comments through the years of working with them helped me learn how to help them. Then my teachers and colleagues whose voices I always hear and use. Without doubt the person who inspired me most in all of my work is my wife, Sonia Leib Abels, whose creative ideas not only inspired me, but also led to the creation of the journal *Reflections: Narratives of Professional Helping.* It aided me and others to understand the importance of the stories that clients and students tell us. I thank James J. Kelly, instrumental in pressing for distance education throughout the world and the person who got the CSULB program off the ground. The authors who wrote chapters for this book have my thanks as well. The continued development of the program at Cal State owes vitality and increased growth to John Oliver, the current director of the Department of Social Work. Finally, I must honor Bea Saunders, now deceased, the former editor of the journal *Social Work* who was willing to take a chance and publish the odd writings of a young social worker in the early 70s, on the future of our profession, much of it science fiction at the time. Thank you all.

Paul Abels
Professor Emeritus

PART 1

The Rise of Distance Education

Chapter 1

THE WAY TO DISTANCE EDUCATION

Paul Abels

REVELATIONS

Distance education in social work is not driven by technology. It is driven by the profession's obligation to educate social workers in a way that will insure their ability to fulfill needed services to persons and communities effectively. It is driven by a recognition of the lack of educational opportunities in more rural areas; and by an ethical imperative to provide opportunities for persons to become social workers who otherwise might be excluded by diversity, economic, or geographic restraints.

I strongly opposed the addition of an interactive distance education (DE) component to our graduate social-work program when faculty was introduced to the idea. Although not quite certain, I believe I was the only objector, or at least the only vocal objector. The presentation explaining the need to offer a social work education to students in locations as far away as 400 miles, during a time of severe shortage of professionally educated social workers in California, was well done. I believed, however, it was not the best way to educate for the profession. I had been invovled in the study of computers since the early 70's and (Abels, 1972) and taught in graduate and undergradu-ate social work programs for about 25 years. I believed that the face-to-face interaction and relationships developed with the teacher and students and among the students would be lost in DE, even in an interactive program. I know these relationships were important steps in the transition from student to professional. Of course, one has to have an educational theory that incorporates these ideas as sound educational principles. I assume most educators do (Perlman, 1967; Reynolds, 1965; Schwartz, 1961).

As the faculty decision-making process evolved, I felt like a character in a melodrama: protecting the students against the foes of good education; I went down in flames. The path that led to my changing my mind, turning me into a supporter of DE, is not the subject of this book, although some reasons reveal themselves in my chapter on teaching in the DE program. Suffice it to say, it began with my contact with the DE students. My conflict is noted here so readers understand that similar to others, including perhaps some of the readers, I questioned the use of this teaching approach in a profession committed to service, connections with persons, and as someone whose own teachers had emphasized the importance of personal relationships and connections in practice and in teaching. All things being equal, I still carry a lingering bias for the traditional classroom's face-to-face-education approach, but unfortunately we live in a society and time when all things are not equal. This is particularly true of students' educational opportunities. The struggle surrounding affirmative action, admission requirements at the college level, and rising tuition costs are three examples of this. The unevenness of education at elementary and high-school levels, which depress some young persons' visions to further their education, is still another.

DISTANCE EDUCATION AS SOCIAL ACCESS AND EQUALITY

As I taught, becoming entwined and engaged in the DE program, talking to the students and some of their families, I came to see how distance education could put into action the profession's mission. DE in social work is not only a medium for the teaching of social work; it also could be a significant force in fulfilling social work's commitment to equality and social justice. By providing a medium for access to persons otherwise unable to further their education, we come closer to meeting our obligation to those left out or marginalized in our society for whatever the reason. In discussing the history of DE, Peters (as cited in Buchanan, 2000) suggests that persons participated in early distance education programs for several reasons:

1. They were denied the opportunity to attend regular schools to acquire the desired qualification;
2. They were poor and socially disadvantaged;
3. They were in ill health [due to the effects of industrialized labor];
4. They were incarcerated;
5. They lived in sparsely settled areas, too far from the university or other educational institution. (p.1)

While these reasons are historically embedded they are relevant to current efforts in the educational milieu. There are two other reasons significant for DE: First, a shortage of professionally trained social workers in many areas, particularly in distant rural areas; and second, because there is a professional obligation to work for the integration of disenfranchised persons. Many groups have been left out of the opportunity structure for geographic and more devious reasons. The lack of options in education extends their disenfranchisement. Almost all of the considerations that Peters (1994) identifies are now, to more or less degree, addressed by some form of DE program.

Social work's historic vision and understanding of the importance of social connections in both social work practice and education make the task more complex then might be required by other professional programs. A general overview of the definition of DE reveals some of the ambiguities DE presents to the social work worldview. Distance education has been defined as the teaching of content in situations where the teacher and the learner are separated by distance, and at times by time. Although there are a number ways DE is implemented, the most advanced programs provide real-time, interactive distance education for the most part by television augmented by e-mail between students and teacher. Though the delivery systems may differ, we face the same questions in teaching through DE as we do in more traditional classroom contexts. How are the connections to be nurtured? How are concepts of relationships enhanced? These questions are made more complex by the lack of face-to-face communication.

What is it we are trying to learn and teach in the profession of social work? How is it to be accomplished? These questions have stirred our thinking since the early days when the idea first emerged that our profession had something unique to offer. To suggest an easy answer to these questions, or to say that we have arrived at the best way to accomplish our goals is not the purpose of this book. Our purpose is to bring to the reader what one approach to learning, DE, has to offer the profession's efforts at quality education, and to examine both its strengths and limitations. To do so we decided to look from the inside, to listen to the voices of those who helped create distance-learning programs. Some are administrators, some the cadre of persons employed to keep the programs on course. How did the site coordinators deal with the teaching, guiding, and political situations faced by their role as distance "guide." How did the faculty deal with the power that television provided? In essence, how does one approach a role that never existed before and for which there are no guidelines? DE is a very new way of learning that presents new challenges along with unexpected opportunities. We hear the voices of students with their own hopes, and doubts, about their own futures.

The authors in this collection share their vision, struggles, and hopes as they work to help students transform themselves into professional social workers. The authors present the workings of distance education as seen by the major actors in this still new and transforming social development. Faculty and students alike are all impacted by the external forces of history, educational theory, technology, myths, research, evaluations, and the politics of community and funding that set some parameters for structure and hopeful success of distance education programs.

ROOTS AND BRANCHES

The education of social workers illustrates that the profession's experience is forever changing, reflecting the context of the times and the difficulties in keeping up with the speed of the change. How different from our early beginnings, when the demands of immigration, poverty, and child neglect called forth volunteers to serve with no more preparation than a belief in people and service. While the problems are similar, increasing calls for training led to sporadic courses; increased knowledge about human behavior and mental health concerns led to the development of courses on the college level and eventually to professional training. Social problems such as immigration, war, the Depression; climatic catastrophes such as the dust bowls; and prejudice and injustice led to actions that called for persons who could deal with such concerns with responses grounded in current knowledge and technology. The foundation of the first social work school supported by the Charity Organizations Society of New York was the culmination of Mary Richmond's efforts to develop a scientific social work. We are now at a point where universities are offering courses on how to teach in distance education (Carnevale, 2003c).

Technology altered many of our views of the possible. And the demands of the possible are that we use current technology on behalf of the people we are committed to serve. If we are to be able to offer needed services by increasing the number of social workers through DE, we are obliged to make use of it—not for the sake of its newness, but for the sake of our clients. This holds true, however, only if it provides professionals with the education they must have to function at the highest levels, an education comparable with traditionally developed accredited programs. The *number* of social workers is not our major concern, although it is an important one. Rather, the concern for quality is vital and the major reason leading to the concerns about comparable professional education addressed by a number of authors in this volume. It is difficult to address in a scientific manner because of the variety of students, educational techniques, and technology used, fieldwork situations and community supports, and the nature of the educational services available to the students. Although possible to establish that the class content and delivery is comparable, the long-term impact of the experience on the students and their ability to practice comparably is more difficult to confirm. All of this is further complicated by the lack of evidence-based practice that may become a major concern for the study of DE in time.

It is not only the pace of change, but the technological and pedagogical differences that raise concern about committing to DE. Psychological factors operate as well, for example, the concept of primacy. The way we first learned to do something is usually the way we continue to do it, unless we learn a better way. These psychological factors act as blocks to innovation, particularly innovation that carries the possible consequences of massive change in professional education. Visualize in your mind's eye the process of DE and then bring forth a picture of your own educational experience. DE is different from the way most of us obtained our social work education. We were schooled to understand the importance of relationship and connections. The personal, face-to-face, intimate interest of an honored, receptive teacher or mentor is a vestigial memory for us in the profession, and not only in social work. A "Mr. Chips" is in the collective memories of most students fortunate enough to have had a mentor-friend relationship. The idea of losing that valuable teaching and learning experience requires openness to the ideas of distance learning when the closest we come to that historical meaningful experience is a conversation on the Web, or viewing that teacher on the TV screen. Certainly that is a loss, which those who are developing distance-learning programs must appreciate and try to mediate. I recall the excitement of the faculty at one of the graduate programs when we found out that our new building had a lounge where students and faculty could have coffee together and chat. Many mutual learnings came out of that experience.

Another concern is economic. It's possible that DE programs are packaged so the instructor might be completely out of the picture in future efforts. A session or entire course can be recorded over the interactive TV and then morphed into presenting the televised session, perhaps followed by discussion in the classroom by a proctor. Thus a change from synchronous learning, where the learner and instructor can interact in real time, will change into asynchronous learning where there is no real-time communication; the student becomes a passive viewer of a presenter (Belanger & Jordan, 2000). The concern is not only with the quality of such education, or that classes only get a particular professor's view locally and perhaps nationally, but could also lead to elimination of faculty positions. There is an increasing pressure on the universities to lower costs; one way is to reduce the number of faculty.

In the DE programs discussed in this book, only interactive television (ITV) programs are highlighted, but it is important to know that other models are possible, and in times of acute financial concerns will be advocated. Prior to ITV there was one way broadcasting of a live program, with responses made by e-mail to the instructor. In some cases the interaction is through e-mail only. A number of classes are offered at universities in this manner. The consequences of all DE programs, the ethics, and the future are discussed in the last chapter.

Educators long advocated that class content is influenced by the nature of the culture and by the group dynamics taking place in the classroom. Some even have advocated that the classroom is a group and work with that in mind. Human-services educators in professions like mental health long understood the special importance of classroom dynamics, or the culture of the class in impacting and being impacted by the content being taught. Two things are vital to the learning experience in a social work class: the content and the teacher's ability to help the student by exemplifying concern for the student and a willingness to accept certain interactions (Northern, 1988; Perlman, 1967; Reynolds, 1965). Many educators maintain that the teacher-student relationship is a paramount factor in the teacher-learner context, and this factor has strong bearing on learning in DE.

Can learning in such a situation be equal or rather comparable to the more traditional teaching situation? These questions are of major concern to many social work educators (Regan chapter) and accrediting agencies such as the Council on Social Work Education (CSWE), which is seeking to gather the information to shape its decisions on distance education. "The Council on Social Work Education has around fourteen master's programs that deliver a majority of their courses using distance education methodologies, with a few that have been in existence for almost 10 years" (CSWE, personal communication, 2003).

One cannot underestimate the magnitude of the change that distance education can bring to the profession and to education in general. Some maintain we became more scientific with the publication of Mary Richmond's *Social Diagnosis* in 1917. Bertha Reynolds pointed out that it took time for the profession to move from a belief that "the main orientation of social work is not authoritative and moralistic but scientific and related to the modern world" (Reynolds, 1965, p. 20). Similarly it will take time for some in the educational profession to accept that distance education and the technology involved are increasingly part of the modern world and that degrees awarded to social workers through distance reflect sound education programs.

Just as the worker asks what is to be "understood" and "done" to help a client, similar questions must be asked of traditional education and the distance learning experience: What is to be understood if we are to help the student learn? What do we need to understand about distance education if we are to make it most useful? What role can distance education play in fulfilling our mission as reflected by the American creed of equality of opportunity, and by Nathan Cohen's idea that social work is humanism in action (Cohen, 1958). Both imply the importance of freedom and equality in our society, proclaiming that all persons should have access to the opportunity to fulfill themselves completely as human beings. Education has always been a major force in realizing this dream of equal opportunity. Not only is one's education level related to economics and status but also to a person's advances in many social contexts and to personal visions. To what degree does TV permit the class opportunities to question the instructor, to discuss common concerns or idiosyncratic positions, and to influence their own education? I believe DE places more power and control in the hands of the teacher but can be used for the benefit of students if the teacher structures material in ways to permit student exploration.

THE OPEN SOCIETY

College education is still out of reach for many in this country, particularly those with the least economic and social capital, as well as for most persons in developing nations. Yet the prospects of higher education have brightened. The evolution of educational technology provides an opportunity for many people to continue their education at home, in areas where televisions and computers are scarce or only provided in centralized sites (Carnevale, 2003a; 2003b)

The terms and definitions *distance education* and *distance learning* are used interchangeably. It emphasizes the idea that the learner and the teacher are separated usually by an extended distance that prohibits live face-to-face contact. Belanger and Jordan (2000) state, "Distance learning can be thought of as education or training delivered to individuals who are geographically dispersed or separated by physical distance from the instructor using computer and telecommunication facilities" (p. 6). In many social work programs where the telecommunication is interactive television, we would use the word *learning* rather than *training*.

Distance education has changed from correspondence courses to advanced degrees often offered by prestigious institutions. Historically, distance education opened up college and technical training for countless numbers of persons. But only in the past decade has it become available worldwide and in a multitude of forms, stimulated by video technology, computer capabilities, and the creativeness of Internet users.

Some early efforts at distance education were meant to broaden one's thinking, or train for specific occupations such as stenography or mechanics, fields that generally did not require higher education. These were home-study courses, offered by private companies. The first university-level correspondence course was given by the University of Chicago in 1892, but it was not until the 1950s that universities started to broadcast college credit courses via television. "Western Reserve University was the first to offer a continuous series of such courses beginning in 1951" (Simonson, Smaldino, Albright, and Zvacek, 2000). It was evident that persons wanted and needed to learn, and ways could be found to serve that need outside the traditional teacher-student-in-classroom format. Economics was not always the reason for not attending college—disability, the need to care for someone at home, or isolation may account for some not attending—it was the lack of funds, and for poor persons and for women, closed doors limited the advantages and fulfillment that college might provide.

Some who saw this as a shortcoming and dangerous to a democratic society recognized the unjustness and consequences of lack of access to education, but little was done to remedy the situation. Change in the education system was slow, in part because of discrimination, economic inequality, and the availability of low-skilled jobs. It was not until the end of World War II that the education system became more open. The GI Bill provided the opportunity for many who could not attend college prior to their service to obtain the funds for college. The next change occurred with the Supreme Court's *Brown vs. Board of Education* decision on separate but equal education which made colleges open their doors. Additional pressures came in the late 1960s and 1970s with the War on Poverty, when the demands were taken to the streets for equal treatment, equal access to jobs, and equal access to education. Where certain fields such as teaching, nursing, and social work had historically been slightly more open to minorities, more lucrative carreers such as law, medicine, and business administration soon drew an increasing number of women and minorities.

University education became the doorway to increased earning and prestige. Demand taxed the institutions that tried to meet the crush as best they could. Realizing that the number wanting education far outpaced classroom seats and that many people needed to work full time, Great Britain initiated a wondrous nationwide distance education program.

In part, the innovators were able to do this because of technology and because of their creative ability to overcome the political obstacles that such a mammoth undertaken must have created. In a sense they were the pacesetters for a massive but quality effort to open up advanced education to all who wanted it.

Verduin and Clark (1991) note, "A decade after its initial operations in 1971, the Open University of the United Kingdom enrolled 60,000 to 70,000 undergraduates a year" (p. 18). It became a model for distance education around the world.

THE CHANGED WORLD OF EDUCATION

The landscape of education has always changed, but never as quickly as in the past decade. The ecliptic change has been brought on by the ubiquitousness of television, the computer, and the synergistic conviviality they provide for the distribution of technology when combined with World Wide Web access. At this moment you are, in fact, participating in distance education. Certainly one of the great technologies (discovered by a number of nations) was the creation of language and writing, and then the technology of the printing press that permitted writing to be duplicated en mass. We might assume that before written language, all teaching and learning took place in person with a teacher and a learner.

Writing created distance education, and books were the "computer" displays by which the learner was able to use the knowledge of a person who was not in direct contact. Today, the TV, computer screen, or audio recording is the display, and radio and cassette tapes were (and still are) distance learning for many of us.

One might just visualize Socrates sitting before a group of students and teaching in order to appreciate the leap we are about to take: to teach worldwide and interact with and be observed by as many students as care to listen and view us.

Distance education, as we will discuss it, relates to the ability of a person in one part of the world to transmit the material to be learned to the expected learners in a distant part of the world by oral, visual, and written means. Distance isn't the most vital factor, since that, as we discussed earlier, is not necessarily new. What is important is that the learning is in real time—instantaneous—and the interaction and response is also instantaneous. For those accustomed to in-class learning with instructors present, absence from the actual face-to-face situation is a crucial differential factor. That the lack of face-to-face, personal connections between teacher and student might retard the learning experience has often been seen as a deterrent to distance education, particularly in fields in which person-to-person connections have been a historical and vital part of the learning-teaching experience. In this chapter we will discuss some of the general perspectives and conundrums that distance education entails, but at one point we will start down the road of social work education. Though we cannot claim to be impartial in our exposition, we will endeavor to let the data speak for itself. In this case the data will be the planners, the teachers, the students, and those charged with carrying out the programs in some way. The major emphasis in this book is on programs that permit the degree to be given to the student based on a total access to distance education and a fieldwork experience. Although there will be incursions into mixed programs of faculty teaching at distant sites, and some limited courses available to students in "traditional" programs, the major effort will be in examining distance education as the total source for the graduate social-work degree. We will also be dealing with the teaching of specific material related to the profession of social work, the special teaching concerns, and explore the technologies that provide the utmost potential for insuring that the course work is not only equivalent to what students would achieve in a classroom with the instructor, but that also leads to similar learning results and consequences.

THE MYSTIQUE OF TECHNOLOGICALLY MEDIATED INSTRUCTION

Don't let the word *technology* get in the way of your reading on. Most people involved in DE are not experts in the technical aspects of the equipment or in the science of computer and television transmission. They have little to do with the hardware of distance learning. This aspect of distance education is usually taken care of by technicians who are well trained in the technology, although you may develop this expertise in time if so desired. The technology that social work needs to pay attention to is the science and art of teaching, the connections they make with the students, the way the course is structured, the organizing principles of the course, and the ability to adapt teaching styles to the distance education milieu. Being on TV does make a difference, to the students and to the faculty. Both planners and faculty are faced with the questions of how best to involve the students, how best to present the material, how best to help them help each other learn, and how best to help them use you, the teacher. Most educators have learned how to deal with these concerns through their experience and exploring the research and available material.

Although much of the research in distance education is related to technology, Palloff and Pratt suggest that the research is really related to pedagogy (p. 18). They cite Phipps and Merisotis (1999) whose statement holds just as strongly for social work education:

> Although the ostensible purpose of much of the research is to ascertain how technology affects student learning and student satisfaction, many of the results seem to indicate that technology is not nearly as important as other factors, such as learning tasks, learner characteristics, student motivation, and the instructor. The irony is

that the bulk of the research on technology ends up addressing an action that is fundamental to the academy, namely pedagogy—the art of teaching. . . . Any discussion about enhancing the teaching-learning process through technology also has the beneficial effect of improving how students are taught on campus. . . . The key question that needs to be asked is: What is the best way to teach students? (p.18)

There are two matters related to technology, however, that are important. The first is that the equipment needs to be both teacher- and student-friendly; the second, usually in the hands of the planners, is that the technology needs to be close to state of the art, which at this point means the use of interactive video technology. Such technology enables the students and the teacher to see and speak to each other and permits all of the students in different locations to hear the interactions and to interact with each other and with the teacher. The nature of the technology in use becomes a factor of importance to the teacher because it makes certain demands on how they perform in the classroom. For example, in certain classroom installations, the camera may turn to the person(s) speaking the loudest. If the broadcast is to two classes simultaneously, the noisier class may get more interaction time with the teacher. In another class setup, there may not be enough microphones in the class and the students might have to share, limiting the amount of time a student might have or reflect how aggressive a student might be in wanting to respond or question. The teacher has to take this into consideration and turn to his/her attention to the other class, or ask if others have something to say and so forth. The skills of the teacher in such situations may not differ from the approaches used in any classes where such problems are not unusual.

The second technology that the faculty needs to consider is the need to be familiar with the computer and its use in the Web and e-mails. In almost all distance education programs, the e-mail becomes a major source of communication with the students related to questions, follow up, suggestions, support, and clarification. In addition it is also used to communicate with the liaison or faculty at the distant site. Such use is mostly ubiquitous and easily learned by an instructor and student who are not yet familiar with its use. The computer has become what Ivan Illich calls a convivial tool, like the telephone and the cell phone, able to be used by everyone who has access to it (Illich, 1973). Ask your children. Some excellent examples of the uses of computers in our social welfare systems are provided by Harlow and

Webb (2003). There are a number of chapters on information technology, the organization of record material, and the use of the Internet for evidence-based practice. (They deal as well with the dark side of the computer, for example the chapter on Internet child abuse.) Clearly there are many forms of distance education as this volume would suggest, but we have limited our work to interactive television in the classroom, not the vast amount of education one can gather from use of the Internet.

Yes, there are sections in various chapters on technology that discusses some of the technology available and what seems to work best for your specific objectives and the limits of the context. The body of the book, however, focuses on the inside of the experience, the actual experiences of teachers, guides, and planners—the bricks and mortar of teaching in a new context. And, yes, the context is a dynamic that both controls and liberates the degree of freedom available to the teacher and to the students. The question of student-centered versus instructor-centered learning arises again, because the students become very dependent on the instructor whose use of control needs careful consideration. The students are in are in unknown territory and this gives the instructor a great deal of influence. Yet there is a paradox; although many more of the students in DE are older and have had more practice experience, they see themselves as learners yet also experienced enough to raise issues that may take the focus off the course and the plans the instructor seeks to fulfill.

THE BIG CONCERN: THE DISTANCE EDUCATION CONTRIBUTION

A statement by the Regional Accreditation Commissions related to electronically offered degree programs notes that "technologically mediated instruction rapidly becomes an important component of higher education" (North Central Association of Higher Learning, 2000). Their efforts are to work toward a balance between accountability and innovation. We suggest that there is another factor for the social work profession that must be considered in balance: the mission of the profession to work for social justice and the ability of the profession to offer the training that provides for that accomplishment.

When distance education was first proposed the question of "comparability" was of major concern. Petracchi (in press) notes the following:

> Since 1995, when the Commission on Accreditation first began dis-
> cussions about the accrediting criteria for distance education, the
> word "comparability" has been lauded as the ultimate criterion for
> distance education; comparability of teaching and classroom expe-
> rience for student at remote sites, and comparability of resources
> for students at remote sites. (p. 344)

One of the vital resources is the availability of adequate field experiences for the distance education student, particularly in rural
areas. It is fair to say that the question of comparability still is a vital
one. Despite research that suggests there is no difference in students'
satisfaction with their fieldwork experiences (McFall & Freddolino,
2000; Petrucchi & Patchner, 2000) a number of students have their
field placements for 1 year in the same agencies in which they work,
although the assignment may be different. This may impact their responses to questions related to their evaluative responses. In their
Michigan University study of field instruction comparing their distance education students with on-campus students, they found that
many of the differences reflected a more positive perception among
the off campus students. In looking at possible explanations for this,
McFall & Freddolino note,

> One feasible explanations is that for both of the distance sites this
> was the first MSW program available to residents close to home.
> There was a considerable demand for admission to the program;
> high motivation among the students, agencies, and communities to
> make the program work; and excitement about being pioneers in a
> new interactive television approach. Thus there may have been an
> inclination to see things more positively. *It is also possible that some
> respondents were afraid to rate these aspects of field instruction more neg-
> atively because of a fear that the program might be terminated* [italics
> added]. By contrast, for the students on campus this was basically
> the traditional MSW program, dealing with the same instructors
> and agencies as MSU and other students had before." (p. 302)

Although they were dealing with reactions to field experiences,
the implications might also hold true for many fairly new social work
distance education programs. In fact, in an earlier article that compared the same reactions to individual courses in the same program
as above Freddolino and Sutherland (2000) state,

> Unlike Thyer and colleagues (1997), students in distance sites did
> not report major differences in the classroom environments from

students on campus. *One possible explanation is that the students at the distance sites may have feared that the program would be discontinued if courses did not receive positive ratings* [italics added] (p. 126)

Obviously there is a need for a great deal of further research on the area of comparability. Most of the research has been of a general nature not reflecting the social work profession's special concerns, and there is little replication of even the limited studies, certainly a statement that is true for the profession as a whole.

It is important to note that the first comprehensive distance education program in social work did not begin until the 1980s. This means that there have been only a handful of programs that have completed their programs and graduated students (in MSW programs). Though research has been done on most of these programs, the sample is still too small, too limited in geographic inputs, too often researched by the providers of the service, and not able as yet to be systematically replicated. We are beholden to limited results, but results that all seem to be directed at showing the success and comparability of the learning experience of traditional classroom and distance education. A more compreshensive view of the research on distance education is presented in chapter 8 by Dr. Potts. Perhaps the only real proof of the success of DE will come when we compare the results of practice with clients by DE and by traditionally educated students following their graduation when their practice skills can be assessed.

DISTANCE EDUCATION MODELS

A number of organizations are trying to develop appropriate models for distance education, which some of these are not educational bodies like universities, they see as their responsibility helping peoples, country's rise from poverty, and are influential in the development of social capital (the World Bank). They offer an important service and some of their approaches have value for social work education. We will concentrate, however, on the models offered for university and professional credit. Though a number of universities have developed their singular idiosyncratic models (Potts and Hagan) there are recommendations to establish a template model that could be incorporated with some modifications by most programs. One such effort is reported by Foster and Washington. Five components are included in their model: (a) accreditation standards compliance, (b) resource requirement, (c) curriculum adaptation, (d) faculty development, and (e) program valuation (p. 148). They maintain that these factors are essential for any effort in the development of a distance education program. The authors go on to discuss each of these items in detail providing a valuable checklist that planners can use as the development evolves. They also maintain that their model is valuable in managing the distance education programs "especially those relying on interactive video technology" (p. 157).

Although theirs is not an actual a model of field practice, McFall and Freddolino developed "action steps" that would serve to meet the fieldwork requirements for students' educational goals in social work distance education programs. These action steps were: developing adequate local resources; creating sensitivity to agency structure and culture; increasing field office resources; and maintaining individual and organizational confidentiality. Each of these actions steps is explicated in depth and together present an excellent guideline for field practice in distance education (2000). Potts and Hagan (2000) suggest a systems model and illustrate its use in a social-work interactional distance education program.

Some of the institutions that have developed DE programs have established formal processes to train the faculty. The University of Pittsburgh has a five step training process, which includes observing a video of the process, a 2-hour workshop, assistance in designing their ITV courses, rehearsal, and observing classes. (CIDDE, 2003).

RESPECT FOR STUDENTS

Some universities have started to help students prepare for the their future classes in DE by furnishing information in the advance of the course. In a piece prepared for the Center of the Study of Bioethics entitled "Technical Requirements for Web Based Coursework" Buchanan (2000) lists what she believes are some of the requirements students are expected to have. These include a personal computer 486 or higher, a later version of Web browser, Windows 98, CD-ROM drive, a minimum 28k modem, and an optional printer. Buchanan also noted the importance of being able to use the Internet and Web-based e-mail.

Buchanan is particularly concerned that there be appropriate resources for the students involve in DE programs and recommends a series of strategies for meeting the needs of students in DE programs.

The strategies run from preparation of course materials, working closely with the librarians involved, and the promotion of interactivity and socialization among students. (Buchanan, 2000).

WHAT LIES AHEAD

We have divided the book into four parts so as to indicate to the reader a general access to topics that might be of interest.

Part 1. The administrative section includes historical efforts and administrative concerns in having DE accepted in our profession. The actual role and experiences of distance-education program administrators, developers, and coordinator are examined.

Part 2 begins with a chapter by Professor Emeritus Frank Raymond, who pioneered distance education in social work. His program was the first in the United States to offer a social work degree through DE. It is important to credit him not only for his foresight, but also for his initiative and ability to overcome the numerous obstacles he faced.

The chapter by Professor Christine Klienpeter illustrates the ups and downs of administering an interactive DE with classes in a number of sites and different universities. Having to negotiate with university officials representing the site's idiosyncratic demands, often from a distance, adds difficulty to the situation. Everyone wants the program, yet not everyone is always on the same page, and some have skipped important pages in their eagerness to start a program. This chapter also includes important information on the type of technology best used for interactive distance education.

Those two chapters are followed by a contribution from a DE liaison, Kathleen Crew. Though not an administrator by intent; Professor Crew served many purposes, from planning to teaching and community resource development. Responsible for dealing with the students on the distant site, she often had to "put out fires" beyond the classroom.

Part 3 deals with the experiences of three teachers in distance education programs. It includes not only their efforts, but the student reactions as well.

Dr. Glezakos highlights how her own experiences influenced her work with the class, their learning, and the appreciation they felt, which led to her being invited by the class and the site university to be their graduation speaker.

I take a slightly different tack, illustrating not only his efforts to develop connections with the students in the classes and help them connect with each other, but also trying to comprehend a puzzle that led to some of the disconnections between teacher and students in one of the classes. A number of theoretical reasons are presented, leaving the reader to their own reflections. This section also presents some of the voices of the students as they grapple with thoughts of the future.

In **Part 4**, two authors examine some of the research done on distance education. Research and program evaluation are important aspects of the undertaking, particularly since questions are raised as to its comparability with more traditional efforts. These questions continue from its inception. A comprehensive review of distance education results is disussed by Dr. Marilyn Potts, and some of the resistance to distance education is discussed by Professor Jo Ann Regan. Dr. Potts' work with students around the thesis requirement is discussed in the Appendix.

Part 5. The final section deals with the future of DE, the influences that it will have and the possibilities of advanced technology. It also examines some of the emerging problems and ethical concerns that DE may present to the profession and the multifaceted impact of technological efforts to educate students through e-mail and computer-related education.

The compilation aims to present the ins and outs of DE, the teaching experience, the learning experience, and administrative planning, challenges, and constraints. Although we have not tried to cover all of the attempts to deal with distance education—which could include everything from telephone calls to computer chat groups—we have dealt with the most technologically sophisticated and state-of-the-art attempts to help social work students obtain their degrees by distance education. We hope the views presented by people on the line in on-line education will give a more complete contextual picture of the uniqueness and continuities of social work education through DE and that it will prove helpful to the reader, whether administrator, teacher, student, or educational dreamer.

REFERENCES

Abels, P. (1972, September). Can computers do social work? *Social Work*, 17(5), 5–11.

Belanger, F., & Jordan, D. H. (2000). *Evaluation and implementation of distance learning: Technologies, tools and techniques.* Hershey, PA: Idea Group.

Buchanan, E. (2000, Spring). Emerging ethical issues in distance education. *CPRS Newsletter, 18*(2), 1–4.

Carnevale, D. (2003a, July 25). NSF head doesn't want to oversee technology program for minority colleges. *Chronicle of Higher Education,* p. A27.

Carnevale, D. (2003b, Sept.). Minn. colleges join forces to teach technology in rural areas. *Chronicle of Higher Education,* p. A43.

Carnevale, D. (2003c, Oct. 31). Learning online to teach online. *Chronicle of Higher Education,* pp. 31–32.

Center for Intstructional Development and Distance Education, Sept. 18, 2004.

CIDDE. (2003). *Interactive television.* www.pitt.edu/~cidde/main/mission.html

Cohen, N. E. (1958). *Social work in the American Tradition.* New York: Holt, Rinehart.

Freddolino, P. P., & Sutherland, C. A. (2000). Assessing the comparability of classroom environments in graduate school education delivered via interactional instructional television. *Journal of Social Work Education, 36*(1), 115–129.

Harlow, E., & Webb, S. A. (2003). *Information and communication technologies in the welfare services.* London: Jessica Kingsly.

Illich, I. (1973). *Tools for conviviality.* New York: Harper & Row.

McFall, J. P., & Freddolino, P. P. (2000). Quality and comparability in distance field education: Lessons learned from comparing the program sites. *Journal of Social Work Education, 36*(2), 293–308.

North Central Association of Higher Learning. (2000). *Statement of commitment by the Regional Accrediting Committee for the evaluation of electronically offered degree and certificate programs. www.ncahigherlearningcommission.org/resources/electronic degrees/index.html.* Retrieved.

Northern, H. (1988). *Social work with groups.* New York: Columbia University Press.

Pallof, R. M., & Pratt, K. (2001). *Lessons from the cyberspace classroom.* San Francisco: Jossey-Bass.

Perlman, H. H. (1967, Spring). ". . . and gladly teach." *Education for Social Work, 23*(2), 41–50.

Peters, O. (1994) Distance education. In D. Keegan (Ed.), *The industrialization of teaching and learning,* (pp.). London: Routledge.

Petrucchi, H. H., & Patchner, M. A. (2000). Social work students and their learning environment: A compararison of interactive television, face-to-face instruction and the traditional classroom. *Journal of Social Work Education, 36*(2), 335–346.

Petracchi, H. E. (in press). Distance learning: What do our students tell us: *Research on Social Work Practice.*

Phipps, R., & Merisotis, J. (1999). *What's the difference?* Washington, DC: Institute for Higher Education Policy.

Potts, M. K., & Hagan, C. (2000). Going the distance: Using systems theory to design, implement and evaluate a distance education program. *Journal of Social Work Education, 36*(1), 131–146.

Reynolds, P. (1965). *Learning and teaching in the practice of social work.* New York: Russell and Russell.

Schwartz, W. (1961). The social worker in the group. *Proceedings of the National Conference on Social Welfare* (2nd ed.). New York: Columbia University Press.

Simonson, M., Smaldino, S., Albright, M., & Zvacek, S. (2000). *Teaching and learning at a distance.* Columbus, OH: Merrill.

Verduin, J. R., & Clark, T. A. (1991). *Distance education: The foundations of effective practice.* San Francisco: Jossey-Bass.

THE HISTORY OF DISTANCE EDUCATION IN SOCIAL WORK AND THE EVOLUTION OF DISTANCE EDUCATION MODALITIES

Frank B. Raymond, III, MSW, PhD

Distance education is now an accepted part of social work education. *Distance education* refers to any formal approach to learning in which the majority of the instruction occurs while educator and learner are at a distance from one another (Verduin & Clarke, 1991, p. 8). This term, which has existed for many years, may have first appeared in the 1892 catalog of the University of Wisconsin (Rumble, 1986). The term was popularized by the German educator Otto Peters (1968) in the 1960s and became commonly used in the United States in the 1980s. Over the past 20 years the use of distance education modalities of various types to deliver social work education has grown dramatically. As the needs of students have changed and as developments in technology have made it easier and less expensive to deliver education, increasing numbers of social work programs, both undergraduate and graduate, have embraced the use of distance education.

HISTORY OF DISTANCE EDUCATION IN SOCIAL WORK

Even though dramatic progress has been made in the development and implementation of distance education modalities in recent years, social work education initially was slow to take advantage of this option for teaching students in remote locations. The end of the 20th century has been called the information revolution, and this era has encompassed radical and pervasive changes in technology. The rapid technological advancement has provided educators an extremely wide variety of electronic tools to assist them in transmitting knowledge to others and has greatly facilitated the delivery of distance education. For a number of reasons, however, social work educators were generally slow and cautious in taking advantage of these advances in technology.

Reasons for Reluctance

In responding to these technological developments, schools of social work educators were more inclined to teach technology than to use technology to facilitate and enhance teaching. That is, schools willingly included in their curriculums content related to information technology, such as the use of computer for research purposes, in agency administration, and enhance client assessment. This content was taught through electives, through required courses, and through integration into other courses. Computer education in social work gradually shifted from an orientation that was primarily pedagogical to one that is focused on application in social work (Cnaan, 1989; Geiss & Viswanathan, 1986; Nurius, Richey, & Nicoll, 1988). Increasingly, schools of social work began to treat information technology skills and concepts as an integral part of the curriculum and a built-in component of core courses, including practice.

In spite of the profession's willingness to teach technology in these ways, for many years there was reluctance on the part of social work educators to utilize these technologies to deliver education. Perhaps this reluctance was because the use of developing technologies for teaching purposes requires paradigm shifts. Educators are generally quick to adopt technologies that support the teacher-student relationship inherent in traditional pedagogical models. For example, technologies such as overhead projectors and video players were quickly adopted. Teaching aids such as these pose no threat to the traditional teaching methods because the teacher remains in control and the same physical spaces are used. However, new technologies such as interactive television systems, multimedia courseware, and the Internet were not as readily utilized by educators to facilitate the teaching and learning processes. The use of such technologies necessitates the fundamental rethinking of the nature of higher education, the roles of teachers and students, the physical environment, and the ownership of intellectual property (Buckles, 1989; Frans, 1993; Mandel, 1989; Pittman, 1994; Raymond & Pike, 1997; Steyaert, Colombi, & Rafferty, 1996). When this type of technology is used, the educator is less a purveyor of information and more a facilitator. The student becomes a more active participant in the learning and more accountable for learning outcomes. During this type of learning process the teacher and student may be separated from each other in both time and space. Such profound changes can be intimidating to educators who are comfortable with traditional approaches to teaching and probably caused many teachers to resist adoption of such technologies.

Another impediment to using technology for distance education purposes was the cost involved. In the early 1980s many types of technology existed that could be employed as distance education mediums, such as audio-video communication systems utilizing telephone lines and closed-circuit television. Unfortunately, most of these systems were very expensive to acquire and operate and were generally unavailable to schools of social work. However, as computer technology developed this modality became a viable tool for providing education to distant sites and expenses were no longer a barrier. The cost of computer technology was greatly reduced in just a few years, making it financially feasible for many schools of social work to use computer networks and interactive computer video systems to provide distance education.

The reluctance of educators in earlier years to use technology for distance education purposes was mirrored by the skepticism of various institutions. Many colleges and universities set up barriers for educators who put forth proposals to deliver education through nontraditional methods. Public authorities who regulate higher education sometimes established stringent requirements for those academic programs that proposed to teach courses through distance education. Private accrediting organizations, such as the Council on Social Work Education (CSWE), were cautious in approving the utilization of technologies to deliver education that differed from the traditional classroom format. With many of these institutions the focus remained on process, rather than on outcomes. Over time, however, these institutions changed their ways of defining program quality. For example, in earlier years accrediting agencies focused their reviews on well-defined criteria concerning matters such as faculty/student ratios, library holdings, and physical facilities. As accreditation evolved, the standards began to reflect a concern with establishing empirical means of assessing quality based on the measurement of outcomes. Most accrediting organizations began assessing programs primarily in terms of how effectively they achieve their stated goals and objectives, regardless of the medium used to deliver education (Raymond & Rank, 2003).

With this new approach to assessing social work education, the Council on Social Work Education (1995) began to encourage schools to be flexible and creative in designing their educational programs. In recent years, the requirements set forth in the CSWE's Educational Policy and Accreditation Standards (CSWE, 2001) and in the Handbook on Accreditation Standards and Procedures (CSWE, 2003) gave schools of social work greater latitude than ever to be self-directed. With these changes, schools were encouraged to determine the educational outcomes they would like to produce and to design the curricula and methods of delivery through which these outcomes could be achieved. Under these new standards it became no longer necessary for schools that wished to implement distance education programs to provide the long, complicated justification and rationale as was necessary in earlier years.

Although social work education, like other academic disciplines, was initially slow to embrace the use of new technologies for distance education, the use of these new modalities has expanded significantly over the years. This expansion was undoubtedly driven by the rapidity of new developments in information technology and the reduction of its costs, as well as the dissolution of previous institutional barriers. Another factor that played a critical role in bringing about the use of distance education technologies was the changing needs of social work students.

The Demand for a New Approach

Although social work education was slow to develop distance education programs, for all the reasons cited above, the changing needs of the students helped motivate schools to consider experimenting with new approaches to delivering education, including the use of dis-

tance education technologies. By the end of the 1990s, the life circumstances of students pursuing degrees in social work began to change
drastically, creating the demand for education to be offered in new
and different ways. Social work training stipends, a major source of
financial aid prior to the 1908s, began to diminish. Consequently,
many persons who wanted to go to school on a full-time basis could
not afford to do so. Furthermore, family obligations, work responsibilities, and other personal situations often made it difficult, if not impossible, for potential students to attend full-time. For those who
lived at distant locations and could not move to the site of the school
of social work, social work education became an impossible dream.
Responding to these circumstances, many schools of social work developed part-time social work programs during the 1980s. At that
time, part-time social work education, especially when offered at distant locations, was a controversial issue. In fact, such programs were
controversial even when programs were offered through the traditional classroom format. Critics of such programs cited potential
problems such as erosion of educational quality, insufficient library
resources, inadequate socialization of part-time students, complications in sequencing courses, and difficulties in developing and overseeing their practicum sites (Task Force on the Future Role and Structure of Social Work Education, 1983).

In addition to the concern about issues such as these, many social
work faculty and administrators believed that accreditation standards would make it difficult to establish off-campus study programs. There was considerable debate in social work circles about the
educational merit of part-time programs (both on-campus and off-
campus). The requirements established by the Commission on Accreditation Standards for such programs were also questioned. Some
academicians believed that the commission was too rigid and unreal-
istic in its demands, even though the commission relaxed its standards for part-time programs as early as 1987. Others believed that
the commission's standards for such programs were not as rigorous
as they should be. Most of these concerns were eventually laid to rest,
however, and schools of social work throughout the United States
began to develop part-time programs in off-campus locations in response to the changing needs of students (Raymond, 1996).

As off-campus social work education programs grew, many
schools found the costs of maintaining these programs to be exces-
sive. Some schools began part-time programs at distant sites and, in
spite of strong beginnings, found that programs could not be sus-

tained for financial reasons. Although the initial group of students may have been large enough to justify the offering of courses at locations remote from the main campus, the high attrition rates often made it economically unfeasible to maintain these efforts. In addition, even the most committed faculty soon grew weary of commuting long distances to off-campus locations. Consequently, schools began to look for other means of providing education to these distant students. Developments in technology provided the answer.

A Pioneering Effort

It was within this historical context that the first distance education program was offered in social work education approximately 25 years ago. The College of Social Work at the University of South Carolina was the first school in the United States to offer its master's of social work degree through interactive closed-circuit television, beginning in 1980. Prior to that time, the college, given its mission to make graduate education available throughout the state, endeavored to achieve this purpose by sending faculty to teach courses to part-time students in two distant locations in other parts of the state. This approach appeared to be somewhat inefficient, however, in that the program was inaccessible to most students throughout this predominantly rural state. The program also proved to be exhausting for faculty who commuted to these remote sites. Seeking an alternative means of serving students, the college decided to experiment with the use of technology that was available through the South Carolina Educational Television system, which makes access channels available to its major state universities and other educational systems. This system utilizes microwave transmission to make interactive closed-circuit television classes available at sites throughout the state. These include university branch campuses, other public colleges and universities, technical schools, public high schools, and libraries.

The college began offering courses in approximately 15 sites throughout South Carolina, with a combined enrollment of approximately 80 students. Because most of these students worked full-time, courses were offered in the evening. Courses were conducted from a studio classroom in Columbia, and students in the distant sites were in live communication with the teacher and with students at other sites throughout the states. In later years, the use of e-mails and listservs was added to enhance the communication and interaction among students and faculty.

Given the novelty of this approach to social work education, it was necessary for the college to obtain permission from its accrediting organization, the Commission on Accreditation of the Council on Social Work Education. Because this was the first time social work education had been offered to distant locations through technology, the commission allowed the program to be offered only on an experimental basis and required that it be thoroughly evaluated over an extended period of time. After numerous reports were submitted to the commission providing empirical documentation of the program's effectiveness, and after a thorough assessment of the program during the college's normal reaffirmation review, the commission granted authorization for the college to make distance education a standard component of its graduate studies.

Since the beginning of the South Carolina program, more than 2,000 students, many of whom live in remote, isolated areas of this rural state, have been able to obtain their master of social work degrees because of the availability of this program. The college's research has demonstrated that these students perform as well academically throughout their course of study as students who complete their entire course work through the traditional classroom approach (Raymond, 1998; Weinbach, Gandy, & Tartaglia, 1984). They have also scored as well as the college's traditional students (and above the national average) on the exam used to license social workers (Raymond, 2000).

Although a microwave transmission system was used to provide distance education in social work at the University of South Carolina as early as 1980, most schools did not have access to technology and to other audio-video distance education until later years. With the growth of networks and the advent of relatively low-priced ICV systems, a significant increase occurred in the number of social work programs offering distance education.

Dramatic Growth in Recent Years

Distance education in social work was advanced significantly during the late 1980s, primarily as a result of the growing use of computer networks and interactive compressed video systems. As the cost of these technologies decreased, more schools began to make use of these modalities to facilitate distance education. In 1993, a national survey of undergraduate, graduate, and combined undergraduate-graduate education programs revealed that 27 of 238 respondents

(11%) were providing curricula through distance education through some type of audio-video communication system (Conklin, Jennings, & Siegel, 1994). When this study was repeated in 1996, 41 of 259 respondents (15.8%) indicated that they were offering courses through such technology. Eighty-three percent of the responding schools had been providing education through technology for less than one year (Siegel, Conklin, Jennings, & Napolitano, 1996).

Because of the growing number of schools offering course work through technology, the Commission on Accreditation of the Council on Social Work Education felt it necessary to address the matter. The commission recognized that the existing standards for accreditation were silent on the subject of distance education. Some consideration was given to the development of new standards. However, the commission ultimately decided to develop guidelines for schools to follow in developing accreditable distance education programs (CSWE, 1995).

Given the encouraging signs from the Commission on Accreditation, more and more schools of social work began to design and implement distance education programs. Schools of social work were also encouraged by developments that were occurring throughout higher education. Increasing numbers of colleges and universities were offering course work and entire degree programs via distance education. By 1997, nearly one quarter of the institutions of higher education surveyed in a representative national sample were offering programs that learners could pursue entirely at a distance. Ninety percent of all institutions with 10,000 students or more and 85% of institutions with enrollments of 3,000 to 10,000 were expected to offer at least some distance education courses by fall 1998 (Gibson, 2002).

During the same years, a plethora of research studies were conducted in higher education in general and social work education in particular regarding the effectiveness of distance education. The findings of the studies across disciplines provided strong support for distance education. Findings revealed that the learning resulting from distance education is as good as or better than learning in traditional classrooms. As early as 1975, a meta-analysis examined a number of research reports that compared courses taught via audio-video communication systems with equivalent courses taught in the conventional classroom looking at all academic levels (Chu & Schramm, 1975). Similar meta-analyses of studies were conducted in the 1980s and 1990s (Verduin & Clark, 1991; Whittington, 1987). In each meta-analysis, it was found that most courses can be taught successfully by audio-video communication systems and that in most cases the learning outcomes of the students who took courses through telecommunications were comparable to, or better than, those of students who took traditional classroom courses. More recent studies have supported these same conclusions (Biner, Dean, & Mellinger, 1994; Ritchie & Newby, 1989; Zirkin & Sumler, 1995).

Numerous evaluation studies were also conducted of social work education programs that used audio-video communication systems to deliver distance education. These studies likewise demonstrated the effectiveness of this medium as measured by factors such as student learning, grades, graduation rates, and student retention (Elliott, Coe, & Mayadas, 1996; Kelley, 1993; Patchner, Petracchi, & Wise, 1998; Raymond, 1996, 1998; & Weinbach et al., 1984). Studies of distance education in social work in more recent years have also revealed that distance education courses and programs are comparable to, if not better than, face-to-face formats. (For an excellent review of these recent studies, see Macy, Rooney, Hollister, & Freddolino, 2001.)

By the turn of the century, the credibility of distance education was firmly established and the delivery of education via technology had become generally accepted as a valid, appropriate, and valuable educational option. It was recognized among schools of social work and by the Commission on Accreditation that distance education via technology was (a) a valuable means of meeting the educational needs of nontraditional students, including those from remote areas; (b) a highly efficient means of delivering education, given the reductions in technology costs; and (c) an effective means of achieving desired education outcomes, as demonstrated by numerous studies. By the year 2000, 20% of social work education was using distance education technologies, an increase of 6% over the previous 5 years (Siegel, Jennings, Conklin, & Flynn, 2000).

The Future

Although interactive compressed video systems have become the most widely used form of technology used to deliver distance education in social work, Web-based courses are now proliferating. Numerous schools of social work are offering courses via that format. Florida State University has begun to offer its entire advanced standing program through Web-based instruction. Although it has been demonstrated that the outcomes of Web-based courses are comparable to those of courses taught in traditional formats, some educators have been reluctant to adapt this format because of the tremendous amount of time required to develop and implement Web-based courses (Sandell & Hayes, 2002).

As schools of social work embrace emerging technologies as a means of delivering education to distant sites, it is likely that they will be supported by the Commission on Accreditation of the Council on Social Work Education. Over the years, the commission has responded professionally to schools' requests to utilize technology to offer distance education, always requiring appropriate justification and evidence of effectiveness. The commission now views the use of distance education technologies as an accepted modality for teaching. In fact, in recent years the commission has become increasingly flexible, not only allowing, but also encouraging schools of social work to utilize new creative methods of teaching students. The Council on Social Work Education's Commission on Educational Policy, working in collaboration with the Commission on Accreditation, recommended significant changes in the Curriculum Policy Statement (which will henceforth be called the Educational Policy and Accreditation Standards or EPAS) (Council on Social Work Education, 2001). The Council on Social Work Education's board of directors approved these recommendations in June, 2001. A significant aspect of the policy is a focus on outcomes, rather than on process. This change has obvious implications for the use of technology to facilitate the delivery of social work education. In fact, the guidelines for distance education adopted by the Council on Social Work Education in 1995 are no longer needed by schools that wish to develop distance education programs. These changes help empower social work educators to develop creative and innovative means of teaching students, including the use of technology.

MODALITIES OF DISTANCE EDUCATION

As the above discussion suggests, as the use of distance education has increased over the years, there has been significant development in the modalities that can be used for this purpose. These modalities, which were referred to in the historical overview, will be described in more detail in this section. The strengths and weaknesses of each method will also be noted.

The earliest distance education consisted of printed and written correspondence by mail. Later, printed materials were supported by audio tapes and video tapes or both. As new developments in technology occurred, the print materials used in correspondence study were augmented by radio or television broadcast signals, but there was no direct real-time communication between the teacher and the learner. In fact, teacher-learner activity was minimal or nonexistent in all of these earlier approaches to distance education (Barker, Frisbie, & Patrick, 1989).

Because of recent developments in computer technology and audio and in video communications technology, the student-teacher interactivity problem has been resolved. Now it is possible for the student and the teacher to be hundreds of miles apart and engage in live interaction with each other and with other students. Additionally, with the advances that have been made in computer technology, such as computer-assisted learning programs and interactive video discs, it is now possible for the teacher to provide an interactive educational experience that does not require real-time interaction with the student. Hence, effective distance education can now be achieved even though the teacher and learner interact while apart from each in time and location (Raymond & Pike, 1997).

There are three primary ways in which new technologies are being used to deliver social work education. These include teaching technology through the use of audio and video communications, through computer-mediated communication systems, and through computer-assisted instruction.

Audio-Video Communications Systems

Developments in audio and video communications (AVC) technology have greatly facilitated interactive distance education. Through use of AVC, students at remote locations can engage in live interaction with the teacher and with other students in real time. This interaction can be achieved in one of several ways, depending on the type of AVD equipment that is available. First, there can be a two-way audio system with no video. This arrangement is similar to an audio teleconference or conference call that includes more participants. Students located at various sites interact with the instructor by using a speakerphone or comparable technology (Raymond & Pike, 1997). A second type of AVC system involves two-way audio and one-way video. Students at distant locations can see the professor and can speak with the professor and other students. The third type of AVC system makes it possible for both two-way audio and two-way video interaction to occur. Through the use of this modality the teacher can see, hear, and interact with the students and, at the same time, the students can see, hear, and interact with the teacher and each other in real time.

The signals can be delivered by a number of means, including telephones lines, satellite systems, cable television, and closed-circuit television. Multiple technologies can be used to produce this level of interaction. These include satellite systems, cable television, closed-circuit television, and interactive compressed video (ICV) systems. (ICV systems will be discussed below, as a type of computer-mediated communication.).

Computer-Mediated Communications

A more recent use of technology to deliver distance education is that of computer-mediated communication (CMC). CMC refers to a variety of communication systems using computers and networks, which includes e-mail and hypertext environments such as the World Wide Web. Distance education can be delivered through use of facsimile, networks, electronic mail, computer conferencing, and other electronic delivery systems. These technologies make it possible for interactivity to occur between the teacher and the student both synchronistically and asynchronistically. CMC has been used for a wide variety of educational purposes including the delivery of undergraduate and graduate courses, seminars, role plays, peer counseling, and self-help groups (Stocks & Freddolino, 1998).

Two of the CMC systems now most widely used in distance education are computer networks and interactive compressed video (ICV) systems. Computer networks, which are collections of computers that are electronically linked and allow information to flow among different computers, have revolutionized education systems. These networks can range in size from local area networks (LANs), which link computers within a small area (such as a university or a department thereof) to wide-area networks (WANs), which connect computers within a large geographic area such as a city or state, to the Internet, which is the largest computer network in the world and connects many of the world's LANs and WANs (Dryden, 1994; Raymond, 2000). Computer networks not only make it possible for students to access data from sources throughout the world, but they also enable educators in both distance education and traditional education classes to interact with individual students at remote sites.

For example, teachers can use electronic mail (e-mail) to communicate with students about teaching assignments, provide feedback on grade exercises, or explain answers to specific questions. Students can submit course assignments to their teachers electronically, ask questions, and obtain feedback from their instructors (Raymond, 2000). These services are being used increasingly in distance education (and in traditional classrooms) to facilitate communication between teachers and entire groups of students who are on their class roles. Messages, notices, and assignments can be posted simultaneously to the entire classes. Discussions, course material, and issues related to learning can also be posted to the list. When used in this manner, the listserv ensures that all members of the class receive the same information, directions, and suggestions from the teacher. Furthermore, the use of the listservs can facilitate more active participation among class members. In addition to general postings on the listserv, class members can send private messages to each other or to the teacher regarding the issue under study (Raymond & Pike, 2000).

For distance education purposes, courses can be offered in their entirety over the Internet. These courses, commonly referred to as Web-based courses, should be differentiated from Web-supported courses. Web-supported courses, either in the traditional classroom or distance education environment, use the Internet to augment and enrich teaching and learning through methods such as e-mail and listservs. In Web-based courses, however, the entire content may be offered online, without any audio-video communication between the teacher and the students. Web-based courses may entail a great deal of asynchronous communication between the teacher and students. For example, student's requests, questions, and comments can be sent, received, and processed at any time. A reported difficulty with Web-based courses is the open-ended demand on an instructor's time because of this asynchronous feature. Another problem is the great deal of time that is required to prepare a Web-based course. Creating and delivering Web-based courses can be even more time-consuming than managing traditional courses (Sandell & Hayes, 2002; Stocks & Freddolino, 1998).

The second most widely used CMC technology is the interactive compressed video (ICV) system. This system is actually a type of audio-video communications (AVC) system in that it allows for two-way audio and two-way video interaction to occur as discussed above. However, the technology used with ICV systems is significantly different from that utilized with other types of AVC. ICV systems combine computers with telephone lines to transmit signals. This technology entails the use of codecs (devices that compress or decompress the signal) on both ends of the digital phone line. With ICV systems there may be a slight delay of sound and some impairment in video quality, depending on the type of equipment that is used (Conklin & Osterndorf, 1995; Freddolino, 1996). ICV systems are now relatively inexpensive to purchase and operate. Consequently, these systems have become the most commonly used form of technology used to deliver distance education in the USA.

Computer-Assisted Distance Education

The third means by which distance education can be delivered is through computer-assisted education. Whereas technology is used as a means to deliver distance education in the two modes of distance education discussed above, in the case of computer-assisted distance education the computer becomes a teaching machine. With computer-assisted education there is no real time interaction between the student and faculty member, but the student interacts with instructional units presented through the computer. The level of interaction can range from low to high, depending on the type of computer application that is used. Interactive computer applications not only allow the student to select a variety of functions within the program, but also make it possible for the student to access information in nonlinear ways. Depending on the application, students can obtain information about their performance from the application (Raymond & Pike, 1997; Raymond, 2000). There are six types of computer-assisted instruction that can be used effectively for distance education purposes: drill and practice, tutorial, gaming, simulation, discovery, and problem solving (Heinrich, Molenda, & Russell, 1985).

Interactive video disks (IVD), one of the first types of interactive computer applications to be developed (Falk & Carlson, 1995), have proven to be highly effective for distance education purposes. Students in remote sites can move through IVD programs at their own paces and schedules. IVD programs normally provide the student with three or four selections, with each choice initiating various video segments, depending on the student's choice. As the student progresses through each component of the program, remedial instruction is provided or feedback is given about the option selected. Students receive immediate positive reinforcement and feedback. Through

IVDs, the distance learner can be exposed to a wide variety of information, including graphics, electronic print, and sound. The student can control the time and length of study of future learning until mastery is achieved. Computer-assisted distance education thus makes it possible to provide individualized learning on a large scale to students in many diverse sites (Raymond, 2000).

There is no doubt that new developments in technology will continue to occur at a rapid pace and that these advances will make social work distance education even more effective, more widespread, and less expensive. Every few months improvements are made in all aspects of distance education technology—the Internet, satellite communications, digital video discs, CD-ROMs, interactive multimedia, and so forth. Developments such as these are actually changing the face of higher education. Commenting on these types of occurrences, Peter Drucker has stated that in 30 years American universities as we have traditionally known them will be barren wastelands. Dryden and Vos, in their top-selling book, *The Learning Revolution* (1999), predict that such profound changes in higher education will occur even faster than Drucker forecasted. Social work academicians will be among those who take advantage of technological developments to discover new and better ways of providing education to students in distant sites.

REFERENCES

Barker, B., Frisbie, A., & Patrick, K. (1989). Broadening the definition of distance education in light of the new telecommunications technologies. *American Journal of Distance Education, 3*(1), 20–29.

Biner, P. M., Dean, R. S., & Mellinger, A. E. (1994). Factors underlining distance learning satisfaction with televised college-level courses. *American Journal of Distance Education 8*(1), 60–71.

Buckles, B. J. (1989). Identification of variables influencing readiness-to-implementation information technology by social work faculty (Doctoral dissertation, Adelphi University, 1989). *Dissertation Abstracts International, 52*, 3652.

Chu, G., & Schramm, W. (1975). *Learning from television: What does the research say?* Stanford, CA: Stanford University Press.

Cnaan, R. A. (1989). Social work education and direct practice in the computer age. *Journal of Social Work Education, 25*, 235-243.

Conklin, J., Jennings, J., & Siegel, E. (1994). *The use of technology as an enhancement to teaching distance education.* Paper presented at Faculty Development Institute, Council on Social Work Education Annual Program Meeting, Atlanta, GA.

Conklin, J. J., & Osterudoy, W. (1995). Distance learning in continuing social work education: Promise of the year 2000. *Journal of Continuing Social Work Education 6*(3), 13–17.

Council on Social Work Education. (1995). *Guidelines for distance education proposals in social work.* Alexandria, VA: Author.

Council on Social Work Education. (2001). *Educational policy and accreditation standards.* Alexandria, VA: Author.

Council on Social Work Education. (2003). *Handbook of accreditation standards and procedures (5th ed.).* Alexandria, VA: Author.

Dryden, G. & Vos, J. (1999). *The learning revolution.* Carson, CA: Jalmar Press.

Dryden, P. (1994). *The PC user's pocket dictionary.* San Francisco: Sybex.

Elliott, D., Coe, J. A., & Mayadas, N. (1996, July). *Distance education: A social development perspective on outreach programs for women and special groups.* Paper presented at the Ninth International Symposium of the Inter-University Consortium for International Social Development, Oporto, Portugal.

Falk, D. R. & Carlson, H. L. (1995). *Multimedia in higher education: A practical guide to new tools for interactive teaching and learning.* Medford, NJ: Learned Information.

Frans, D. J. (1993). Computer diffusion and worker empowerment. *Computers in Human Services, 10*(1), 15–34.

Freddolino, P. P. (1996). Maintaining quality in graduate school social work programs delivered to distance sites using electronic instruction technology. In E. T. Reck (Ed.), *Modes of professional education II: The electronic social work curriculum in the twenty-first century* (Tulane Studies in Social Welfare, Vol. 20, pp. 48–63). New Orleans, LA: Tulane University.

Geiss, G. R., & Viswanathan, N. (1986). *The human edge: Information technology and helping people.* New York: Haworth Press.

Gibson, C. C. (Ed.). (2002). *Distance learners in higher education.* Madison, WI: Atwood.

Heinich, R., Molenda, M., & Russell, J. D. (1985). *Instructional media and the new technologies of instruction* (2nd ed.). New York: John Wiley & Sons.

Kelley, P. (1993). Teaching through telecommunications. *Journal of Teaching in Social Work, 7,* 63–74.

Macy, J. A., Rooney, R. H., Hollister, C. D., & Freddolio, P. P. (2001). Evaluation of distance education programs in social work. *Journal of Technology in Human Services. 18*(3/4), 63–84.

Mandel, S. F. (1989). Resistance and power: The perceived effect that computerization has on a social agency's power relationships. In W. LaMendola, B. Glastonbury, & S. Toole (Eds.), *A casebook of computer applications in the social and human services* (pp. 29–40). Binghamton, NY: Haworth.

Nurius, P. S., Richey, C. A., & Nicoll, A. E. (1988). Preparations for computer usage in social work: Student consumer variables. *Journal in Social Work Education, 24,* 60–69.

Patchner, M. A., Petracchi, H., & Wise, S. (1998). Outcomes of ITV and face-to-face instruction in a social work research methods course. *Computers in Human Services, 15*(2/3), 23–37.

Peters, O. (1968). New perspectives in correspondence study in Europe. In O. MacKenzie & E. L. Christensen (Eds.), *The changing world of correspondence study.* University Park: Pennsylvania State University Press.

Pittman, S. W. (1994). An exploratory study of the diffusion of instructional computing innovation among social work faculty. *Dissertation Abstracts International, 55,* 152.

Raymond, F. B. (1998, July). Providing social work education and training in rural areas through interactive television. Paper presented at the Annual National Institute on Social Work and Human Services in Rural Areas, Fort Collins, CO. (ERIC Document Reproduction Service No. ED 309 910).

Raymond, F. B. (1996). Delivering the MSW curriculum to non-traditional students through interactive television. In E. T. Reck (Ed.), *Modes of professional education II: The electronic social work curriculum in the twenty-first century.* Tulane Studies in Social Welfare, Vol. 20, pp. 16–27. New Orleans, LA: Tulane University.

Raymond, F. B. (2000). Delivering distance education through technology: A pioneer's experience. *Campus-wide information systems,17*(2), 49–65.

Raymond, F. B. & Pike, C. K. (1997). Social work education: Electronic technologies. In R. L. Edwards et al. (Eds.), *Encyclopedia of Social Work: 1997 Suppl,* (pp. 19, 53–62. Washington, DC: NASW Press.

Raymond, F. B., & Rank, M. (2003). *Preparing for accreditation in social work education: The self-study and the site visit.* Alexandria, VA: Council on Social Work Education.

Ritchie, H., & Newby, T. J. (1989). Classroom lecture/discussion vs. live televised instruction: A comparison of effects on student performance, attitude, and interaction. *American Journal of Distance Education, 3*(3), 36–45.

Rumble, G. (1986). *The planning and management of distance education.* London: Croom Helm.

Sandell, K. S., & Hayes, S. (2002). The web's impact on social work education: Opportunities, challenges, and future direction. *Journal of Social Work Education, 38*(1), 85–99.

Siegel, E., Conklin, J., Jennings, J., & Napolitano, S. (1996). *National survey on distance learning in social work education, preliminary data.* Manuscript in preparation, New Haven: Southern Connecticut University, Department of Social Work.

Siegel, E., Conklin, J., Jennings, J., & Flynn, S. (2000, February). *The present status of distance learning in social work education: An update.* Paper presented at the Annual Program Meeting of the Council on Social Work Education, New York, NY.

Steyaert, J., Colombi, D., & Rafferty, J. (Eds.). (1996). *Human services and information technology: An international perspective.* Aldershot, England: Arena, Ashgate.

Stocks, J. T. & Freddolino, P. P. (1998). Evaluation of a world wide web-based graduate social work research methods course. In F. B. Raymond, L. Ginsberg, & D, Gohagan (Eds.), *Information Technologies.* (pp. 51–69). Binghamton, NY: Haworth Press.

Task Force on the Future Role and Structure of Graduate Social Work Education. (1983). *Strategic issues in the future role and structure of graduate social work education in the United States.* Seattle University of Washington School of Social Work.

Verduin, J. R., & Clark, T. A. (1991). *Distance education: The foundation of effective practice.* San Francisco: Jossey-Bass.

Weinbach, R., Gandy, J., & Tartaglia, L. (1984). Addressing the needs of the part-time student through interactive closed circuit television: An evaluation. *Arete, 9*(2), 12–20.

Whittington, N. (1987). Is instruction television educationally effective? A researcher review. *American Journal of Distance Education, 1*(1), 47–57.

Zirkin, B. G., & Sumler, D. E. (1995). Interactive or non-interactive? That is the question!!! An annotated bibliography. *Journal of Distance Education, 10*(1), 95–112.

PART 2

Planning and Administration of Distance Education in Social Work

Chapter **3**

MANAGING THE DISTANCE: DISTANCE EDUCATION ADMINISTRATION

Christine B. Kleinpeter, MSW, PsyD

This chapter will present a perspective of distance education (DE) from the viewpoint of a faculty member who taught and served as the distance education coordinator in a large urban program that was designed to serve the needs of rural communities that did not have access to master's level social work education. The administration of this DE program was located within the Department of Social Work at the main campus, and all students enrolled through the University College and Extension Services. All DE sites were located on state university campuses, which operated under the direction of a central chancellor's office. The funding for this program was a combination of federal IV-E and student tuition dollars.

Outlined in this chapter are the challenges and rewards of planning and implementing a DE program. The roles of both on-site and main campus administration are reviewed. Issues of collaboration with multiple institutions, quality of the DE program, accreditation standards in social work education, and university reward structure for faculty will be discussed.

43

BACKGROUND

In 1998, 44% of all higher education institutions offered DE courses, compared with 33% in 1995. Additionally, the number of degree programs offered through DE increased from 690 in 1995 to 1,190 in 1998 (National Center for Education Statistics, 1999). Currently, 20% of social work programs utilize DE, which represents an increase of 6% in the past 5 years (Siegel, Jennings, Conklin, & Flynn, 2000). Societal changes contributed to the growth of DE in the United States: (a) the increased requirements for higher education for career advancement; (b) the demand for flexible scheduling by nontraditional students; (c) the general shift in the public's attitude from one that views education as a youthful pursuit to one that values lifelong learning; (d) the growing requirement in many professions for continuing education; (e) the emphasis that many employers place on specific competencies, rather than on degrees, in hiring; (f) the shift by educators from teacher-centered education to student-centered learning; and (g) the increasing awareness among educators that students vary greatly in their learning styles (Mehrotra, Hollister, & McGahey, 2001). These factors have generated a great deal of interest in DE by institutions of higher learning.

DE also stimulated cooperation among 2- and 4-year institutions of higher education. Collaborations of several institutions have been formed to deliver advanced degree programs (Potts & Hagan, 2000). Proponents argue that DE will help create a more efficient deployment of the nation's educational resources by facilitating the sharing of individual institutions' specialized expertise. Thus, institutions of higher education will not be obliged to spread their resources across so many disciplines and specialties, but will be able to focus them in selected areas (Mehrotra et al., 2001).

DE literature suggests that by the 1990s, the costs of equipping classrooms for iteractive television (ITV) had dropped substantially (Mehrotra et al., 2001). The availability of this technology persuaded many educators to give serious consideration to establishing DE courses or programs. By the late 1990s, many colleges and universities were offering entire degree programs through interactive television (ITV).

A number of studies have found that the educational outcomes of DE courses are comparable with those taught in traditional classrooms (Biner, Dean, & Mellinger, 1994; Potts & Hagan, 2000; Zirkin & Sumler, 1995). These positive outcomes led to changes in the accrediting bodies' standards that address these new technologies and recognize the advantages of DE for fulfillment of institutional missions. DE provides invaluable service to students previously denied access because of geographic or scheduling difficulties. Additionally, DE shows great promise in the areas of continuing professional education, personal enrichment, and lifelong learning (Mehrotra et al., 2001).

CHALLENGES AND REWARDS

In 1994, the Council on Social Work Education's Commission on Accreditation introduced standards of comparability, mandating that (DE) programs must meet the same standards as on-campus programs (Wilson, 1999). This resulted in numerous studies that evaluated the educational experiences and achievements of DE social work students and found that they are at least comparable to those of traditional students (Coe & Elliott 1999; Petracchi & Patchner, 1998; Potts & Hagan, 2000). Student evaluations also indicated that satisfaction levels in DE equivalent to those obtained for on-campus programs (Coe & Gandy, 1998; Freddolino & Sutherland, 2000; Hollister & Kim, 1999) There were mixed results regarding practice methods courses; some studies found practice students less satisfied with DE courses than on-campus students (Thyer, Polk, Artelt, Markward, & Dozier, 1998; Thyer, Polk, & Gaudin, 1997).

Criticisms of DE have also been raised concerning the classroom experience, the institutional supports for students, and the costs of equipment and faculty and staff salaries (Mehrotra et al., 2001). The experience of DE students has been a concern, particularly, in the area of conducting experiential classroom exercises. Some authors (Mc Henry & Bozik, 1995) have indicated that DE classrooms lack adequate interaction both between sites and within each site. Smith and Wingerson (2000) found that ITV results in a decrease in reception of nonverbal communication. The authors suggested that the loss of nonverbal communication may lead to significant misunderstandings between the sites in a DE classroom.

The costs of a DE program using interactive television (ITV) include the initial costs of equipment, and costs of paid technicians at each off-campus site. The use of site coordinators as assistant instructors in the classroom adds the cost of instruction by providing, for example, one faculty member in addition to two site coordinators to each linked classroom which serves approximately 40 students (Potts & Hagan, 2000). Faculty are also paid overtime for the additional preparation time involved and travel time to visit each site during the semester (for each single course in the DE program, faculty are paid for two courses) (Potts & Hagan, 2000). Institutional supports, including library resources and student health and disabled student services, are difficult to provide at off-campus locations (Moore & Kearsley, 1996). This difficulty is overcome if the DE sites are located at other university campuses (Potts & Hagan, 2000). Thus, students have access to the local library at their off-campus site. Financial arrangements can be made between the host institution and the off-site institutions in order to cover the costs of medical or other student services. This is accomplished through the use of a contract that provides for fee-for-service reimbursement to the off-site institutions by the host institution (Kleinpeter & Oliver, 2003). Therefore, students can access health, counseling, and disabled student services provided at the DE sites. Because of the added costs of the DE program, some universities have used grant monies in addition to charging DE students higher tuition in order to meet the costs (Potts & Hagan, 2000).

Although the challenges of offering a DE program are substantial, the rewards are many. Students who attain a degree using a DE program are usually living in rural areas, have family responsibilities, and are employed (Moore & Kearsley, 1996). For these students, moving to a traditional social work program located in an urban area is unlikely. Therefore, they are able to attain career goals in social work that they might not otherwise attain without a DE program. Potts and Kleinpeter (2001) found that DE students located jobs immediately after graduation, nearly 75% held jobs in the public sector, and nearly 50% were working in public child welfare. These are gratifying outcomes when one realizes the magnitude of the need for social workers, particularly those working in the area of public child welfare. DE may be an important avenue used by universities to address the workforce shortfall in social work agencies.

LOCAL ON-SITE ADMINISTRATION

Some DE programs in social work address the challenge of classroom environment with the use of site coordinators (Blakely & Schoenherr, 1995; Hagan, Wilson, Potts, Wheeler, & Bess, 1999). Site coordinators conduct experiential exercises, lead discussions, proctor exams, and manage the classroom environment at the off-campus sites. More discussion of site coordinator roles is included in the next chapter of this book.

At California State University Long Beach (CSULB), site coordinators were used in the DE classrooms as teaching assistants, academic advisors, and field work coordinators (Hagan et al., 1999). In this capacity, they provided valuable support to faculty teaching over ITV. Faculty members varied in the way that the site coordinators were used to accomplish educational goals, depending on the course objectives and their teaching style. Site coordinators had a very important role in teaching practice courses that included monitoring of skill development and application of social work practice theory.

The site coordinators have primary responsibility for the development and implementation of field education in DE programs (Hagan et al., 1999). Black and Cohen (1997) outlined the role of site coordinators in field education including the development of field placement sites, negotiation with prospective field instructors, assignment of students to placements, and monitoring the overall operation of the field work courses. The involvement of these local community experts was an integral component in the development of local placements. Field placements are not readily established in most rural areas due to lack of appropriate master level supervision. Networking assisted in the development of the field placements by fostering the local social service community's interest in the DE field program (Bess, 2003).

A primary function of the site coordinators was to provide assistance to students experiencing difficulties. Site coordinators advise DE students regarding administrative tasks, such as registration, financial aid, and graduation requirements. Therefore, they need to be familiar with all of the policies and procedures of the MSW program and of the main campus. In their role as academic advisors, site coordinators are an important link to provide information to students from the main campus regarding matriculation issues.

MAIN CAMPUS ADMINISTRATION

Moore and Kearsley (1996) identified strategic planning as one of the critical tasks that administrators must perform in preparing for a DE program:"formulating goals and objectives for the institution; balancing aspirations with currently available resources; assessing changes in student, business, or societal demands; tracking technology alternatives, and projecting future resource and financial needs" (p. 196). In planning for a DE site, several factors need to be considered and a feasibility study must be conducted in order to determine if a particular DE site is viable. The primary areas to be considered include: technology, funding, local faculty, student services (e.g., library, health, and disabled-student services) on the university side; and in the local community, the availability to fieldwork placements and field instructors, and potential students must be identified (Kleinpeter & Oliver, 2003). Additionally, logistics of course offerings (part-time/ full-time) and days of the week when potential students are available to attend school need to be identified.

Institutional supports including library resources and student health and disabled student services are difficult to provide at off-campus locations (Moore & Kearsley, 1996). This difficulty can be overcome if the DE sites are located at other institutions of higher learning (Potts & Hagan, 2000). Thus, students can access the local library at their off-campus site, as well as the use of the main campus library accessed through the Web. Financial arrangements can be made between the main campus and the off-site institutions in order to reimburse the costs of medical or other student services. This can be accomplished through the use of a contract that provides fee-for-service reimbursement to the off-site institutions (Kleinpeter & Oliver, 2003). Therefore, students can access health, counseling, and disabled student services provided in their local community. Because of the added costs of the DE program, some institutions have used grant monies in addition to charging DE students higher tuition in order to offset the costs (Potts & Hagan, 2000).

Strategic planning activities begin with an assessment of the available resources for a DE program at both the host institution and the partnering institutions. The off-campus site resources include both university resources, as well as community resources. At the host campus, administrative resources are needed in the area of planning and implementation of the program.

In order to provide a DE program in social work, a proposal to the Council on Social Work Education currently is required of the host institution. That proposal must outline the proposed sites, curriculum model, funding sources, staffing patterns, technology used, evaluation plan, and needs assessment. DE currently is considered an experimental program; and as such, requires CSWE approval for each program cycle. In addition to approval from the accreditation body, a proposal for the funding source may also be required. The CSULB program was partially supported by a grant, federal IV E funding (Potts & Hagan, 2000). Administrative time at the host institution was required to complete the funding and accreditation proposals.

Equipment and technician time is required of the host institution in preparation for the delivery of a DE program. At CSULB, 75% of the curriculum was delivered over ITV while 25% was delivered in face-to-face instruction (Potts & Hagan, 2000). Technician time was required to test the compatibility of the host institution's equipment with the proposed DE sites' equipment. In some cases, new equipment was purchased to prepare either the host or the off-campus site prior to the start of the program.

Staffing patterns must be planned to accommodate the increased workload of administrators, faculty, and staff at the host institution. Some portion of administration time is required of the director of the social work department, the director of field education, the graduate advisor, and the admissions director. Many schools of social work have added a distance education director to assist with the coordination of registration, financial aid, student services, technology, and to mange the training and supervision of the site coordinators. Managing the recruitment and matriculation of DE students takes additional time and must be accounted for in the administrative budgeting of time and financial resources.

Many DE programs are offered through extended education. Administrative time is required on the part of extended education administrators to facilitate student enrollment, maintain contracts with faculty for salary, schedule technology and technicians, assist with marketing, and manage the budget (Kleinpeter & Oliver, 2003). If courses are Web-based or Web-enhanced, then additional technical time is needed to assist instructors with the use of the Blackboard or Web-CT technology.

Faculty resources are of prime consideration in the planning process of a DE program. At CSULB, faculty who teach in the DE program are required to travel to each DE site two times per semester (Potts & Hagan, 2000). Faculty meet with students for office hours and provide professional socialization activities for DE students during those visits. Courses are offered on Saturdays to accommodate working students; therefore, in addition to the availability to travel, faculty must also be available to work on weekends. Because one course counts for two in the CSULB model, faculty in the DE program are less available to teach at the host institution; therefore, additional faculty are needed to run a DE program than would be necessary to teach the same number of on-campus courses.

In addition to assessing its resources in terms of equipment, staffing, accreditation approval and funding; the host institution needs to assess the potential DE site. It must be able to provide the host institution with compatible equipment, classroom availability, technician availability, library resources, student services, and administrative time to coordinate the program (usually through extended education). Additionally, some faculty time at the local site may be needed for courses that require hands-on instruction such as computer statistics or field seminar courses. It is also important to have a "point-person" at the potential DE site who can assist in identifying the stakeholders within the university and within the local human service community.

At this point in the process, a formal needs assessment is conducted at the potential DE sites (Kleinpeter & Oliver, 2003). Two primary methods have been employed to accomplish these tasks. First, a meeting is held with primary stakeholders in the potential DE site with both university personnel and community representatives. Local university personnel, usually include senior administration, extended education, technology services, student services, and a departmental representative, that is, the point person (e.g., chair, BSW, or sociology department). Local community representatives include social service agency directors and practitioners. Administrators from the host campus usually include the director of the department of social work and the distance education coordinator. The purpose of the meeting is to gain a mutual understanding of the community need for a program and the university resources available to support a DE program at both the DE site and the host campus.

Second, a needs assessment is conducted in the form of surveys. One survey is aimed at local human-services agency directors, primarily asking the number of available field instructors to supervise students' fieldwork experience, and number of potential students the agency could support. A second survey, is aimed at potential students asking primarily issues related to completion of BSW or related degree, completion of prerequisites, and availability for taking courses (e.g., Saturdays). This data is complied to assess feasibility of a potential DE site.

The meeting with stakeholders and the needs assessment are opportunities to discover potential barriers to program development. If the barriers cannot be resolved, this may be a point to revisit the institutional goals and resources available for the DE program. The potential DE site or the host institution may not have the available resources necessary to overcome a potential barrier (e.g., not enough potential students or field work agencies). If no barriers are identified by the needs assessment, then marketing strategies are planned to begin advertising the DE program and offering community orientations to assist potential students in fulfilling prerequisites and making application to the program.

The strategic planning tasks listed above are labor intensive and usually take place 1 to 2 years before the students begin their first day of class. Students will need orientation to the DE program with special emphasis on how to access library resources; the faculty will need orientation on teaching strategies used in DE; and the site coordinators will need initial and ongoing orientations to provide them with tools for each of their required tasks. CSULB offers a 3-year, part-time model, therefore much of the contracting with field agencies and matching students with field placements takes place in the first year of the program. Orientations for field instructors and field liaisons take place in years 2 and 3 of the program.

Because of the complexity of the job, site coordinators at CSULB are brought to the main campus for training for 2 days each semester of the program. The orientations outline curriculum that will be covered during the upcoming semester and the coordinators' role as teaching assistants in presenting this aspect of the curriculum. Information is also presented that is needed for field work development at each stage of the program from development of placements though resolution of student problems that occur in the field. Their role in assisting students at each phase of matriculation, such as preparing forms for advancement to candidacy or designing a plan for academic improvement for probationary students must be explained. Site coordinators are given an opportunity to resolve problems that may exist in communication between the local campus and the host campus at these meeting times. Site coordinators provide valuable insight in the resolution of problems that may be unique to their job, which is unlike any administrative or faculty assignment on the main campus. It is an ongoing administrative responsibility of the main campus to provide support and supervision to the site coordinators. At CSULB, this is the primary responsibility of the distance education coordinator, with assistance from the director of the department of social work, the director of field education, the California Social Work Educational Center (CalSWEC) project coordinator, and the graduate advisor.

LESSONS LEARNED

As distance education coordinator, I encountered several barriers (Kleinpeter, 2003).

Faculty Workload and Compensation

When the new DE program was established, teaching a DE course meant responsibility for the 63 students connected by ITV over three sites across the state. Additionally, it meant committing to four weekends away from home to visit the students and provide professional socialization activities in their communities. It also involved preparation of visual materials, usually PowerPoint presentations for each lecture. Unfortunately, the faculty did not foresee the added workload, so the first proposal did not include additional pay or time off. This problem was resolved by the second cycle of the DE program when faculty voted to compensate a DE course at double the rate of an on-campus course. With the compensation issue resolved, many more faculty members were willing to teach in the DE program. This was an important barrier to overcome as the Council on Social Work Education requires that social work programs use the same faculty in the DE program as in the on-campus program, as well as equivalent textbooks and assignments.

Lack of Integration with the Main Campus

DE students were required to take a writing proficiency exam on the main campus rather than at their local campus. This was not possible due to travel distances involved, so the DE coordinator was sent to each DE site to administer a writing proficiency exam during our first two cohorts. By the third cohort in 2001, this issue was resolved by the passage of a new university policy, which allowed substitution of the GRE Writing Assessment test. This solution was a cost savings for the DE program, as well as time saving on the part of the DE coordinator.

Collaboration

One of the most difficult aspects of the DE program was collaboration with other campuses. Each campus was structured with budgets specific to that campus. Therefore, there was no way to share credit for student enrollment (i.e., FTES) with another campus. This would have benefited the rural campuses that were in need of FTES to increase their budget allocation. Additionally, faculty at the rural campuses were needed by our program to teach specific courses, such as Computers in Social Work, which is taught in a computer laboratory. Similarly, faculty workload is not shared across campuses; therefore, if we hired a faculty member from the rural campus to teach one of our DE courses, it was as an overload for that faculty member. This was difficult as many faculty members found that they were not able to manage the overload, although they verbalized that they would enjoy teaching a DE course if it counted as part of their regular workload. This made it difficult to staff the DE program as we had several courses (about 25% of the curriculum) that needed to be taught in a face-to-face format. The difficulty was twofold: (a) the ability of a faculty member to manage a part-time (3-unit overload) in addition to covering their full-time commitment at the rural university; (b) there were no other faculty members to replace them at their university, even if there had been a way to share the workload between campuses. The barrier was overcome primarily by offering DE courses on Saturdays and over the summers when some rural faculty members were able to manage the additional workload.

Quality

Faculty on the main campus had many reservations about the initial use of ITV for teaching social work courses, particularly for practice courses. During the planning phase, a consultant who had experience with DE was enlisted (i.e., social work dean) from another school of social work. Primarily, he answered questions that were raised by faculty about the quality of the education that students in DE programs receive. He was an excellent resource as his institution had been involved with DE for many years. His visit smoothed the way to a positive faculty vote in favor of adding the DE model to our large urban MSW program.

In addition to concerns about the quality of the DE program, faculty were also concerned whether we could manage to maintain the quality of the on-campus program due to draining our faculty resources for the DE program. Some faculty members felt that the drain to our on-campus program was too high a cost to pay. This was compounded by the faculty vote to count the DE courses as a double load, which indeed meant that when professors taught in the DE program, they were even less available to teach on-campus students.

These concerns were not unfounded. At times, the issue of faculty drain from the main campus was evident in our evaluation materials, when DE students did better and were more satisfied with their course than the on-campus students. When program administrators saw this, we made greater efforts to mix experienced and inexperienced faculty over all of our program models. As the DE coordinator, I am always tempted to pull our most experienced faculty into DE. I reason that students are at a disadvantage if they are unhappy with a course as they have no opportunity to transfer to another section. However, on-campus students experienced the same issue one semester, when all of the research methods course instructors were put into DE thesis committees. This left no one who had taught this preliminary course to serve as thesis advisors to the on-campus students.

Accreditation

In 1995, the old standards for accreditation were in place and initiating a DE program required special permission from CSWE. A detailed proposal had to be written to explain the method of delivery for each course with a justification as to why it would be effective. Additionally, how fieldwork would be set up and supervised from a distance had to be outlined. The proposal explained what evaluation plan would be used and yearly reports to CSWE were included in the plan. The proposal was written 1 year prior to the students beginning their courses.

The basis for the evaluation was to compare on-campus with DE students and show equivalence. This method was criticized as being a deficit model, seeking to show that DE students are as good as on-campus students, which supposes that on-campus teaching is superior (Macy et al., 2001). Little testing had been conducted of whether traditional teaching was effective. Many social work faculty and administrators questioned the CSWE about why DE programs were held to higher standards than were on-campus programs.

Many of these questions may be answered by the focus on outcome assessments beyond student grades and faculty course evaluations. When outcome measures are established to cover each course and the overall goals of the MSW curriculum, it should answer many of the questions about technology that are currently raised. If students can meet the standards set on the outcome assessment tool, then the method of course delivery will no longer be an important focus.

Funding

Funding for the DE program at CSULB is a combination of student tuition and grants. We are fortunate in California to have the hardware for ITV already installed at our state-supported campuses. Additionally, we have federal IV-E funding though the California Social Work Educational Center (CalSWEC) grants to support students and programs designed to educate the workforce in public child welfare. This means that students who work for the agency that houses the child welfare function in each county are eligible to receive reimbursement for tuition, books, and travel to allow them to complete an MSW degree. This grant pays for the costs of the program not covered by student tuition, including coordinators, administrators, travel expenses, equipment, and clerical assistance.

The CalSWEC funders then require that the university recruit at least 50% of the students from public child welfare employees. This is difficult when recruiting students from rural areas, as there may be a smaller workforce to recruit from than in urban areas. A complicating factor is that counties differ in how they support their employees in this process. Some counties allow students to work part-time during years two and three of the program so that they may complete the required 16 hours of fieldwork. This makes it difficult for students, as they may need additional funding to cover living costs. Other counties pay their employees full-time salaries while they are completing their fieldwork requirements. Although this is not a decision that the university makes, it does mean that some students have been unable to complete the program due to financial reasons.

University Reward Structure

In DE programs faculty who are not yet tenured need to be protected from engaging in activities that are not valued by the university reward structure. For example, when evaluated for tenure and promotion, I had been involved with teaching and administration of the DE program and had written extensively about both. At that time, no inclusion was made in the university's policies regarding tenure and promotion about the use of technology in the faculty evaluation process. My materials presented for tenure and promotion looked unusual in that most of my articles had focused on DE, and most of my service contributions related to socialization of DE students, advising DE students, and program development toward new social work programs at other campuses. I think one of the most difficult aspects of evaluation of the service contributions of individuals involved in DE is the lack of visibility on one's own campus or in one's own community. Since I spend at least 20% of my work life out of town teaching or overseeing the DE program, my evaluation materials reflected less on-campus and local community service than faculty members who were not involved in this amount of required travel.

The lack of clear guidance from the university in this area created uncertainties for the RTP Committee and at times became stressful for me. Our university is aggressively working on developing policies that will reward faculty for their work in the area of technology. As more faculty members engage in the use of new technologies, it will be important for faculty reward structures to recognize these important contributions.

CHALLENGES UNRESOLVED

At times, it is not possible to resolve or overcome a barrier in a way that makes the process of developing a DE program possible. Two such examples follow. In the first case, student recruitment had taken place for 1 year at a campus that had invited our participation in the development of a DE site. The support of the local community stakeholders was strong, and there seemed to be sufficient interest in the potential student pool to recruit a cohort. All the preliminary approvals from our funder and accreditation body were in place. However, the low number of applications prevented the site from being successful. Inquiries about further marketing attempts to recruit additional students to the application pool met with resistance from the campus. It was never clear to me what had blocked the usual admission process with DE students at that site. However, it became clear at a later point in time that priorities may have changed and loyalities may have shifted in the 1–2 year period required to begin a new site, as history demonstrated that another institution was invited to provide a DE program in that local area.

In another location, a similar difficulty arose with the development of a new site, with a slightly different issue. In this second community, a similar amount of time had passed related to securing funding, accreditation, and student recruitment. The academic institution also had strong interest from the local social-service community and a large pool of potential students. In this case, the dollar amount of reimbursement for use of the distance education equipment was the barrier that could not be resolved. The program could not go forward at that location and had to be moved to another academic institution. The puzzle here was that many similar institutions had received the same reimbursement and were able to deliver the service over many years. This was the first time for our program that the amount of reimbursement to other campuses blocked our ability to work in collaboration.

In both examples, as an outsider to the other institutions one cannot know the budget constraints, the priorities of the campuses, or any changes in key administrative personnel that may also be important factors in the development of a collaborative venture involving multiple academic institutions. The dilemma for the main campus offering the DE program is to decide what number of DE sites they can support. When preparing staffing and the budget, it is imperative to build in flexibility to account for the reduction in the number of sites due to unexpected circumstances.

CONCLUSIONS

DE is exciting because of the opportunities it provides the student and faculty to learn and develop new skills. Like all exciting innovations, technology itself is not what drives DE administrators, but rather the knowledge that the technology is a bridge to connect people who can work together on common goals. In my case, it was the development of a program that was able to meet important goals (i.e., increasing the number of MSWs in California and assisting campuses in the development of new MSW programs) that drove me. It is exciting to plan and implement new programs that meet the needs of a diverse group of communities. Although the tasks are challenging, the benefits are well worth the costs.

REFERENCES

Bess, G. (2003). A distant perspective on distance coordination. *Reflections: Narratives of Professional Helping, 9*(2), 68–72.

Biner, P., Dean, R. & Mellinger, A. (1994). Factors underlying distance learner satisfaction with televised college-level courses. *American Journal of Distance Education, 8*(1), 60–71.

Black, J., & Cohen, B. (1997, March). From a distance: The partnership between field education and distance education technology. Paper presented at the Annual Program Meeting, Council on Social Work Education, Chicago, IL.

Blakely, T., & Schoenherr, P. (1995). Telecommunication technologies in social work distance education. *Professional Development: The International Journal of Continuing Social Work Education, 6*(3), 8–12.

Coe, J., & Elliott, D. (1999). An evaluation of teaching direct practice courses in a distance education program for rural settings. *Journal of Social Work Education, 35*(3), 353–366.

Coe, J., & Gandy, J. (1998). Perspectives from consumers (students) in a distance education program. *2nd Annual Technology Conference for Social Work Education and Practice, Conference Proceedings* (pp. 91–98). Columbus: University of South Carolina College of Social Work.

Freddolino, P. (2003). Back to the beginning: My first year in distance education. *Reflections: Narratives of Professional Helping, 9*(2), 27–34.

Freddolino, P., & Sutherland, C. (2000). Assessing the comparability of classroom environments in graduate social work education delivered via interactive instructional television. *Journal of Social Work Education, 36*(1), 115–129.

Hagan, C., Wilson, G., Potts, M., Wheeler, D., & Bess, G. (1999, Winter). The role of the site coordinator in a social work distance education program. *Journal of Continuing Social Work Education, 2*(3), 11–18.

Hollister, D., & Kim, Y. (1999). Evaluating ITV-based MSW programs: A comparison of ITV and traditional graduates' perceptions of MSW program qualities. *3rd Annual Technology Conference for Social Work Education and Practice,* Conference Proceedings, Charleston, SC. Columbus: University of South Carolina School of Social Work.

Kleinpeter, C., & Oliver, J. (2003). Site development in a distance education program. *Journal of Technology in Human Services, 22*(1), 75–84.

Kleinpeter, C. (2003). Swimming up stream: The experiences of a pioneer in distance education. *Reflections: Narratives of Professional Helping, 9*(2), 10–16.

Macy, J., Rooney, R., Hollister, C., & Freddolino, P. (2001). Evaluation of distance education in social work. *Journal of Technology in Human Services, 18*(3/4), 63–84.

McHenry, L., & Bozik, M. (1995). Communicating at a distance. A study of interaction in a distance education classroom. *Communication Education,* *44*(4). 362–372.

Mehrotra, C., Hollister, D., & McGahey, L. (2001). *Distance learning: Principles for effective design, delivery, and evaluation.* Thousand Oaks, CA: Sage.

Moore, M., & Kearsley, G. (1996). *Distance education: A systems view.* Belmont, CA: Wadsworth.

National Center for Education Statistics. (1999). *Distance education at post-secondary education institutions: 1997V98* (NCES 2000-013). Washington, DC: U.S. Department of Education.

Petracchi, H., & Patchner, M. (1998). ITV versus face-to-face instruction: Outcome of a two-year study. Paper presented at the Conference on Information Technologies for Social Work Education and Practice, Charleston, SC.

Potts, M., & Hagan, C. (2000). Going the distance: Using systems theory to design, implement, and evaluate a distance education program. *Journal of Social Work Education, 36*(1), p. 131–145.

Potts, M., & Kleinpeter, C. (2001). Distance education alumni: How far have they gone? *Journal of Technology for Human Services, 3/4*(18), 85–99.

Siegel, E., Conklin, J., Jennings, J., & Flynn, S. (2000, February). *The present status of distance learning in social work education: An update.* Paper presented a the Annual Program Meeting of the Council on Social Work Education, New York, NY.

Smith, P. R., & Wingerson, N. W. (2000, August). Effective communication "across the screen" for social work distance education. Paper presented at the 4th Annual Technology Conference for Social Work Education and Practice, Charleston, SC.

Thyer, B., Polk, G., Artelt, T., Markward, M., & Dosier, C. (1998). Evaluating distance learning in social work education: A replication study. *Journal of Social Work Education, 34,* 291–295.

Thyer, B., Polk, G., & Gaudin, J. (1997). Distance learning in social work education: A preliminary evaluation. *Journal of Social Work Education, 33,* 363–367.

Wilson, S. (1999). Distance education and accreditation. *Journal of Social Work Education, 35*(3) 326V330.

Zirkin, B., & Sumler, D. (1995). Interactive or non-interactive? This is the question! An annotated bibliography. *Journal of Social Work Education, 10*(1), 95–112.

Chapter 4

WHICH HAT DO I WEAR?
THE MULTIFACETED ROLE
OF THE SITE COORDINATOR
IN DISTANCE EDUCATION

Kathleen Crew

As site coordinator for California State University (CSU) Long Beach, Distance Education Program on the CSU Hayward, Contra Costa Branch campus, both social work and distance education technology are part of my every day life. "High tech" provides remarkable opportunities for social work students throughout the Northern California Bay Area to receive graduate instruction. Students sit in a specialized classroom with four large TV screens, microphones hanging from the ceiling, and cameras zooming in and out, capturing the class as a whole and showing close-ups of individual students sitting in cushioned chairs behind several rows of tables. Each Saturday two faculty members at Long Beach present their lectures on TV, with simultaneous broadcast to CSU Humboldt and CSU Hayward. One class is presented in the morning, the other after lunch. Each is a three-hour session. The four screens enable a variety of camera views, creating a virtual classroom, in which students at both sites can interact with each other and the faculty member.

Although basic lectures are similar in content to regular classes, technology affects the actual presentation and delivery. Professors must remain stationary in front of the camera, and frequently use overheads in extra large type. Both faculty and students understand the need for adaptations in classroom etiquette. Noises such as paper shuffling or whispering to colleagues are amplified by microphones and become distracting. Students who speak in class must identify themselves by name and location and some faculty require name cards in front of the student. The actual schedule and rhythm of the class is affected. As in the usual class session, the cameras might be scanning the room as the students enter, but the class starts when the instructor calls the class to order no matter what else is happening in the local classroom. Punctuality is an important aspect of the session, as the two sites may be in different states of readiness. If there are disturbances off-camera that might disturb the session, such as two students talking to each other, as site coordinator I would attend to it quickly, as the instructor would not be aware of what he or she cannot see or hear.

Instructors actively facilitate the interaction from site to site, seeking comments from each in an attempt to equalize airtime. The initial experience of distance education can be disorienting. With professors in one location and students in several others, it is not uncommon to lose track of the geography because all of the interchange occurs in a virtual classroom but the camera only picks up one class at a time. The instructor cannot see all the students at one time. Of course this would not be the case if only one class was being taught.

THE FACILITATING FUNCTION

Given all of the adaptations that distance education requires, the site coordinator becomes pivotal. It is in this position that the cornerstone of good social work education and practice rests. It is in good part through the site coordinator's efforts that the relationships are formed and maintained with the students, the hosting campus officials, faculty, staff, and local social welfare community. In this arena of distance education, "high tech" must intertwine with "high touch" for the program to be successful.

The relationship function of the site coordinator is unique, varied, and multifaceted. Given that the Distance Education MSW Program is a 3-year program, the site coordinator becomes a significant and central person in the students' lives. The site coordinator facilitates building connections between students and development of the culture of the cohort. The skills of social work are exemplified by the site coordinator's actions.

The program does not enroll new students each year, so the same students stay together throughout the program cycle. A major task is to provide a conducive learning atmosphere, building trust and encouraging development of the group as a cohesive unit. All the students have been away from college for a number of years. Although enthusiastic about returning to school, issues of self-confidence are frenetic. In the first semester the focus is to aid students gain the understanding that the college has confidence in their capabilities of doing graduate level work; that they will pass their first midterms; that they can actually write a 10-page paper (or more) and if necessary make use of the tutoring services to assist in polishing and increasing their skills. What they believe about themselves and their capacity to learn has a significant impact on retention. It is at this early stage that the site coordinator plays a central role of reassurance and support. Although there are similar supports in the regular classroom setting, the partnership in distance education is a unique one. The students take all but one class together for the next 3 years. The lack of choice means that they have to come to terms with the situation. It also affects their sense of independence, as they have no choice of class or teacher. Often it is the group's strength, the students' connections, and the site coordinator's connections and actions that serve them during critical times. Because the program is located away from the home campus, the usual cadre of faculty and staff available is not.

THE ADVISING FUNCTION

The site coordinator also serves as academic advisor. Though the main campus graduate advisor is accessed by phone, the physical presence of the site coordinator has a more significant meaning, which becomes particularly important after the first midterm. Some students receive a grade below B. The site coordinator, as *the* faculty representative, must consult with them to create a constructive plan to achieve at a higher level. This requires the coordinator's knowledge of the host campus, as well as local resources, and the ability to assist students in analyzing their learning needs and issues. It also requires contact with the instructor if additional work is required. This advising relationship is significant. It is difficult for the student—who often has been a successful professional for many years—to adjust to a grade less than desired or anticipated. They question their ability to be a learner again. Sensitivity, reassurance, and respect are crucial to encourage the student's academic growth.

It is not uncommon for students to seek counseling relationships with the site coordinator. In this context the coordinator is able to express concern and support, while simultaneously maintaining appropriate professional boundaries, and referring the student to community resources if necessary and agreed upon. Once again the connections of the site coordinator with the community often insures a thoughtful referral. It is important that confidentiality be maintained and respected. Students share personal information in the hope that the site coordinator will act as their advocate with faculty or administrators on the main campus as well. The coordinator can aid the students by suggesting strategies to manage the larger academic system on their own behalf. There are many instances, however, where the site coordinator is in a position to facilitate the communication between the students and individuals on the main campus.

THE EDUCATION FUNCTION

At all times, the site coordinator must be ready to function as an educator. Given that the coursework is offered via the technology, there are occasions when the communication systems unexpectedly break down. It is not uncommon for the coordinators to facilitate as much of the class content as possible on behalf of the faculty member who is not physically present. In addition, professors may request the students to do interactive exercises during the actual course, and it is the site coordinator's job to coordinate these. The Boy Scout motto, "Be Prepared," is applicable to working in a distance learning classroom. It is important for the site coordinator to have the course outline and in some cases has material provided by the faculty that might be helpful in emergencies.

A less apparent, yet significant function of the site coordinator is that of a role model. Given that the individuals who hold this position already have earned their MSWs, the students are inclined to emulate the coordinator's sense of professionalism, often requesting their opinions about educational and fieldwork concerns. Boundary issues apply here as well. Good judgment is required to share what is appropriate with the students, yet caution must be maintained so as not to become inadvertently involved in areas that are best referred to others. The site coordinator's relations with the classroom faculty also help in understanding boundary issues, which might differ among faculty. The site coordinator's perspectives on the normal adjustments and challenges of graduate social work education may reassure students. This function often provides an anchor for the students as they develop their own sense of professional identity.

The position of the site coordinator can be best understood as a hub. The college itself, the individual faculty members, the administration, the hosting campus, and the students all revolve, and intersect, around it. It is an interesting reality that while the site coordinator must be familiar with and facilitate many job functions, most often there is no one at the main campus who understands all the hats the site coordinator must wear. Along with purchasing paper clips and Scotch tape, it is not uncommon for the site coordinator to be viewed in the local community as the unofficial dean of the program. There are meetings with the host campus and with local county and agency administrators. At the same time, the site coordinator is not in a high-level position on the organizational chart in the social work department. This reality often creates a tension that is sensitive to manage and not easily recognized by the department. It can lead to a sense on the part of the site coordinator of having many responsibilities, but marginal authority. The administrative model used in the academic world can also create frustration for the site coordinator, who must intersect with multiple individuals at the main campus, all of whom may have a different opinion about how to handle certain situations.

Communication is a significant function of this position. The variety of people needing to make connections and exchange information is at times very challenging. Although there is frequent technological sharing, the U.S. mail remains the most common means of receiving course materials and university documents, though the availability of express or overnight mail is extremely useful. Professors are sent their exams to grade in this fashion as the tests are often given quite close to the date that grades are due. Major stress occurs if materials do not arrive in timely fashion, particularly since classes are only held once a week and students come from a range of geographic locations.

A number of last minute emergencies have occurred, including the collection of an Express Mail envelope containing final exams by my 80-year-old neighbor who wanted to be helpful. She did not understand the meaning of urgent on the envelope and kept it in her home for 3 days, presenting it to me at 8 a.m. on Saturday morning as I left for campus, frantically arranging with my counterpart in Humboldt to fax me the exam so that I could make copies for the students on campus.

Given that the distance education program is a guest of the host campus, accessing the resources that are available to regularly enrolled students is not always possible. The distance education program in Hayward is on the semester system. The host campus is on the quarter system. This affects the opportunity to use the library, the computer lab, and the cafeteria. The site coordinator is often in the position of trying to facilitate alternatives on the students' behalf.

FIELD DEVELOPMENT AND COORDINATION

One major responsibility of the site coordinator is to develop the fieldwork program. It is in this function that network-building skills with a wide range of social service agencies are required. The site coordinator becomes an emissary of the host campus, representing the social work department from a distant campus in the local community. Many professionals are unfamiliar with the concept of distance learning and the unique constellation of the 3-year, part-time model. It is incumbent upon the site coordinator to gain the confidence of the local community agencies and to clarify their concerns and questions on behalf of establishing fieldwork options. It is a time-consuming task that includes initial calls, connecting to the appropriate personnel, triaging by phone, and meeting directly with the agency directors and social work staff to assess the possibility of learning opportunities for the students.

In the capacity of fieldwork developer, the site coordinator is also responsible, under the direction of the main campus, for determining the appropriate match of student to agency and communicating this decision to both. Given the level of investment that students have in their fieldwork assignments, this can be a delicate task. Here again, the relationship of the site coordinator with the students is central.

COMMUNITY SUPPORT AND DEVELOPMENT

Another significant task in network building is in development of an advisory board that represents the community at large. The board membership reflects a strong statement to the local community of the commitment of the main campus to diversity and inclusiveness on a variety of levels. The site coordinator must develop a board that builds confidence in the host campus and in its ability to provide excellent education to the students who will practice social work in the local area. Thus, the selection of individual board members is important. Along with the site coordinator, these individuals become the spokespersons for the program in the professional community and build its credibility.

Recruitment is another important function of the site coordinator. This function filters throughout all the others, in that whatever the site coordinator is doing represents the program at large. It is not uncommon for individuals to approach the site coordinator to learn more about the distance education MSW program. There are various organized information days in a variety of locations that require the site coordinator to present the details of the program and provide information about the admission process. Although individuals are frequently referred to the Long Beach campus, the site coordinator wears the hat of an admissions officer on many occasions.

AND MORE

Building positive relationships with faculty members is a cornerstone for success in distance education. It is difficult to define all that is entailed in this function. The site coordinator is responsible for disseminating course materials, proctoring exams, and getting them to the professors expeditiously. Faculty members often rely on the site coordinators to be their eyes and ears more directly in a classroom than they are managing over the technology. Professors visit the distance education sites twice per semester. At those times, the site coordinator arranges for the students to have both social time and office hours with the faculty member, again facilitating relationships. When an occasional faculty member is hired locally, the site coordinator serves as a liaison between the main campus and the instructor, orienting the professor to the policies and practices of the social work department.

THE IMPORTANCE OF PERSONAL CONNECTIONS

A distinct challenge for the site coordinator is developing a network of colleagues. Although the faculty and staff at the main campus are helpful and available, there are no specific counterparts in Long Beach with the exact duties. Given the nature of the job itself, there are no colleagues in the local community. By virtue of the position, the truest colleagues that exist are other sites coordinators throughout the state. At times this creates a sense of loneliness and isolation that may result in the site coordinator's flying by the seat of his or her pants and hoping that the pants don't get worn out. Colleagues at the other sites, however, are available by phone and e-mail and willing to provide support whenever it is requested.

A particular challenge in the job of site coordinator is building relationships with the main campus. It takes time to establish rapport and develop a sense of collaboration when one sees other employees infrequently and one's only contact is by phone or e-mail. The lack of informal moments and face-to-face interactions make this difficult. As I was hired, there was an additional stress. The September 11 attacks occurred several days after our first Saturday class, which led to significant delays in flying site coordinators to the main campus for orientation and training.

The combinations and permutations in the role of a distance education site coordinator are many. Qualities such as flexibility and resilience definitely apply, and a sense of adventure is also a requisite. The overriding function of this position, however, remains that of a relationship builder. The network of connections developed between and among the site coordinator and the students, the local community, the fieldwork agencies, and CSU Long Beach Department of Social Work determine the level of success for everyone. Connecting the sites by technology is significant. Connecting with the people who are involved in each aspect of the educational process is crucial.

PART 3

Teaching in Distance Education

Chapter 5

THE TRIBULATIONS AND REWARDS OF DISTANCE EDUCATION TEACHING

Agathi Glezakos

> In the house of education there are many rooms... and intimate face-to-face colloquy need not be held in all of them.—James Russell Lowell

Prior to the 1990s, my knowledge of the distance education programs that operated under the auspices of colleges and universities was limited. However, my impression of their learning outcomes in the education of social workers was somewhat negative. The experience of completing my master's in social work (MSW) in the early 1960s convinced me that good professional social work education is only possible in a program where instructors and students have face-to-face interactions.

During the past 5 years, I had the opportunity to teach MSW students in a distance education program. This experience has brought me to recognize the valuable role that distance education programs can play in the training of social work professionals, and it has enhanced my appreciation of the contribution these programs make to the quality of social work manpower and of service delivery.

The proliferation, quality, and contributions of distance education social work programs have been documented (Faria & Perry-Burney, 2002; Huff, 2000; Petracchi & Patchner, 2001; Resnick & Anderson, 2002). It is projected that advances in educational technology, coupled with an increasing need for professionally trained social workers, will promote the expansion of distance education programs (Freddolino, 2002; Heitkamp, 2000; Sheafor, 1996). It is thus critical that we, as teachers in the profession, come to grips with the future that is in store for us, and also that we take the time to assess the benefits, as well as the potential pitfalls, that this mode of teaching presents.

I begin this chapter by providing a brief account of the events that influenced my decision to become a teacher; I then go on to describe my experiences of teaching in a MSW distance education program. The content of the chapter is almost exclusively subjective, though I do offer some recommendations on the basis of my experience. In particular, I hope that my personal account triggers the interest of some social work educators and researchers to ascertain empirically possible universal aspects of this mode of social work education.

HOW I CAME TO BE A TEACHER

My own teachers have stirred my imagination and broadened my aspirations. My interactions with them encouraged me to dream ever greater dreams and to change my goals.

My third- and fourth-grade teacher, Mr. Nickolas Pappas, arrived in our war-ravaged village in post–World War II Greece. He made me believe that it was worthwhile to form ambitions and to make a difference in the lives and outlook of eager young people. Margaret Stewart, MSW, an American instructor during my undergraduate studies, encouraged me to apply for a Fulbright so that I might one day teach at my alma mater (Pierce College in Athens). Dr. Helen Northen, School of Social Work, University of Southern California; and Dr. Earl V. Pullias, Department of Higher Education, School of Education, University of Southern California urged me to aspire to a PhD and a teaching position at the university level.

MY EVOLUTION AS A UNIVERSITY TEACHER

My teaching experience at the university level began in 1973 when I taught my first class, Introduction to Social Welfare, in the Department of Social Work at California State University, Long Beach (CSULB). Since then, over the course of 30 years, I have taught undergraduate and graduate courses as a part-time and a full-time lecturer and as a tenure-track faculty member.

In the early 1970s the Department of Social Welfare at CSULB had a small faculty and an accredited undergraduate program. I taught the Introduction to Social Welfare course with a practicum, the Human Behavior and the Social Environment course (HBSE), micropractice courses (social work practice with individuals and groups), and field seminars. When the department developed the MSW program, in 1986, I began to teach some of the graduate courses in the same subject areas. For the past several years, I have taught only graduate courses, including elective courses and thesis. I taught these courses to on-campus and distance education students.

TEACHING FROM A DISTANCE OVER INTERACTIVE TELEVISION:

In the fall of 1998, I accepted a 1-year full1time lectureship opportunity to teach in the department's distance education program, which was about to begin its second 3-year MSW cycle with a new cohort of students at four different rural and semi-rural sites.

By reading intradepartmental reports about the program, and in conversations with the department's director, the director of the distance education program, and colleagues who had taught in the distance education program, I gained a basic understanding of what was involved in teaching a class via interactive television: the mode of technology used to transmit a lecture and to dialogue with the students and the site coordinators. I reviewed the literature on distance education and found documented evidence from survey and comparability studies that the students in distance education programs performed as well as on-campus students (Forster & Rehner, 1998; Freddolino, 1998; Patchner, Petracchi, & Wise, 1998). Nonetheless, some of my colleagues expressed concerns about the effectiveness of this form of social work education, as well as about the draining effects the distance education program might have on the department's overall resources. Similar concerns were also raised by some authors in the literature. In light of the above, I was not surprised to find myself skeptical about this new teaching assignment. My skepticism was exacerbated by my limited knowledge of computers, and of technology in general. I began to prepare myself psychologically and pragmatically for the coming year.

Other than brief sessions with the staff at the university's studio and a discussion with the director of the distance education program who has experience in teaching over interactive television, I had no formal instruction in how to approach this new mode of teaching. I entered this uncharted territory as instructor for a course in Human Behavior and the Social Environment (HBSE) with 31 students at two different sites: Humboldt State University and California State University, Bakersfield. During that same term, I taught a section of the same course to 24 students on campus. Even though I had taught this course to several on-campus groups of MSW students in the past, I had spent significantly more time preparing instructional material for the delivery of lectures to the distance education students over interactive television. My lectures in the on-campus classroom were enhanced by the use of this material. At the end of the academic semester, I had found no differences in the learning outcomes between the two groups of students in their final grades. This finding was similar to the findings of studies that compared learning outcomes of distance education and on-campus students (Coe & Elliott, 1999; Kleinpeter & Potts, 2000; Patchner et al., 1998; Petracchi & Patchner, 2000).

The following semester, spring of 1999, I taught the second course in the HBSE sequence to 36 students in the other two sites of the department's distance education program: California State University, Channel Islands, and California State University, Chico. In the fall of 1999, I returned to teach a foundation course in generalist and multicultural social work practice to these two sites. During both semesters I taught similar courses to on-campus full- and part-time students of almost equal size groups. I reconnected with all four distant sites during their second summer in the program when I taught one of the two elective courses the students were required to complete before graduating. The focus of the elective was on assessment and treatment in direct social work practice and there was simultaneous interaction with all four sites.

Three years later, when a new cohort of students from three different sites (Humboldt State University; California State University, Hayward; and California State University, Channel Islands) was admitted into the program, I returned to teach the two courses in the HBSE sequence during the first year, alternating sites between the fall and spring semesters. During their second year in the program, I taught again the foundation course in generalist and multicultural social work practice to students at one site in the Fall semester and a course in social work practice with individuals and families to students at the other two sites during the spring semester. As was the case with the previous cohort of students, I taught the HBSE and the foundation courses to on-campus students as well. The course in social work practice with individuals and families is designed on the basis of concentration. The focus of the course for the distance education students was on practice with children, youth, and families while the focus of the practice course I taught on campus during this semester was on older adults and families.

In summary, my experience in teaching distance education in the MSW program has consisted of two 3-year cycles. The first cycle included a total of 67 students at four different sites. The second cycle included a total of 49 students at three different sites. My teaching load consisted of five different courses.

The experience of teaching distance education over interactive television with intermittent site visits was quantitatively and qualitatively different from teaching in the conventional classroom setting. The preparation of instructional material called for a different level of creativity and new organizational skills. This, in combination with the time spent to visit the different sites at least twice during each academic semester, was taxing on my time. The presentation of the instructional material to a distant audience was periodically disrupted due to problems with the technology. Losing visual contact with students, not being able to maintain ongoing audio communication, and needing to resort to a back-up plan implemented by the site coordinators created an emotional upheaval. With each semester, however, these hurdles became more manageable and the experience of this mode of teaching became more rewarding.

LESSONS LEARNED

I can now say with confidence that my teaching experience in distance education has presented me with challenges that I had not previously encountered in the classroom, and it has brought equally novel rewards as well.

Challenges

Classroom environment. I have learned that striving to transmit knowledge and create a classroom environment conducive to learning over interactive television when you are almost computer illiterate is a major, anxiety producing undertaking. Technology permeates all aspects of academia today; nonetheless, there are still those who, like me, do not feel fully at ease with the very latest instructional tools. Teaching in a distance education program requires a level of comfort in front of the camera, ability to be flexible with the day's teaching agenda when the technology fails, and skill in the use of teaching aids such as PowerPoint. I tackled this challenge by working to improve my computer and PowerPoint skills, and by accepting the necessity of developing back-up plans for the inevitable times that the technology might fail to function.

Instructor's teaching style. Delivering a lecture over interactive television will probably not be compatible with every instructor's familiar or preferred teaching style. Teaching over interactive television requires that the instructor be positioned so that he or she is visible to the students at all times. For the instructor who is accustomed to moving around the classroom and who prefers close physical proximity to the students, this mode of teaching can feel confining and restrictive. I found that having to make adjustments to my teaching style affects my emotional state in the classroom and has the potential to diminish the enthusiasm with which I approach each class meeting. The early awareness of these counterproductive effects, a conscious and systematic effort on my part to adapt to this new style of teaching, and each semester's cumulative experience helped increase my level of comfort as I delivered my lectures from a confining position.

Shared classroom environment. In the more traditional teaching-learning environment, the classroom is the domain of the teacher and of the students. When one teaches over interactive television in a distance education program, the teaching-learning environment probably includes several other individuals. In my situation, the "classroom" environment was shared with a site coordinator and a technology assistant. The technology assistant was either a staff member of the university's media department or a student assistant. During some semesters, the technology in my classroom was managed by a series of student assistants. The presence of these individuals can be intimidating to the neophyte instructor. In addition, lectures are usually taped, and a copy of the tapes is kept by the individual sites. What the instructor says, how he or she says it, and what transpires between instructor and students in the course of each class meeting becomes part of the public and permanent record. This arrangement not only raises the question of ownership of your "intellectual property" but it may also alter one's familiar teaching style. I caught myself being more reserved, reticent, and less spontaneous than I am usually in the conventional classroom setting. Much of this was altered with each successive semester and I found it easier to submerse in my familiar teaching style.

Obstacles to effective communication. The physical distance between the instructor and the students can interfere with the successful resolution of any misunderstandings in their communication. Instruction over interactive television can hinder the students' level of active participation in classroom discussions. In my case, for instance, I have found that my dry sense of humor is usually appreciated by the on-campus students, but more than once it has been misinterpreted by distance education students. A challenge that I faced, then, was how to change my response to some student questions to prevent such misunderstandings. This situation was ameliorated somewhat during my visits to the individual sites where there was opportunity for face-to-face exchanges and for socialization on a more personal level. Nevertheless, more than once noncomplimentary comments appeared on the student instructor evaluations that were never made by on-campus students.

Student evaluation of teaching effectiveness. Another obstacle that the physical distance creates is the restricted opportunity to assess the effectiveness of your teaching as the semester evolves. In face-to-face, ongoing individual and collective interactions with on-campus students, it is easier to make this assessment. In the distance education program, this assessment is more difficult because your ability to gauge the students' responses is somewhat impaired by the intervening medium of the technology. If your familiar paradigm of pedagogy is not congruent with the students' expectations, learning and professional development objectives, and life situations, discontent in the classroom can linger for some time before this incongruity is brought to your attention by one or more vocal students or by the site coordinator. It might also happen that you learn about the incongruity only from student feedback on the students' instructor evaluations at the end of the academic semester. This was my experience with students at two different sites in two different semesters. (What was particularly puzzling in these situations was the significant difference in the student ratings between two cohorts at two different sites that I was reaching simultaneously.) Because poor instructor evaluations can have ramifications for faculty retention, tenure, and promotion, one should perhaps agree to teach in a distance education program over interactive television only after careful consideration.

Course content and site-specific practice issues. Distance education sites have primarily been in rural or semi-rural areas where there are no major universities with an undergraduate or graduate social work program. This created some difficulties for me, as I tried to maintain identical course standards for the on-campus and the distance education students. This dilemma is more pronounced in direct practice courses. Content in these courses needs to be relevant to the students' internship experiences. The practice issues of the distance education students are often quite different from the urban communities in which the on-campus students primarily work and intern. Furthermore, there have been differences among the different distance sites. I became more aware of site-specific practice issues from the students' input during class discussions, individual student e-mails and/or phone conversations, and from the content of student term-papers. Knowledge of the ethnocultural and socioeconomic characteristics of the community in which the distance education site is located and on-going dialogue with students, site coordinators, and field instructors can help the instructor meet this challenge.

Effects of demographics on student expectations. Studies comparing demographics of age, work, and family responsibilities of on-campus and distance education students indicate that greater numbers of distance education students tend to be employed full-time—many of them in responsible positions in a wide array of health and human services—to be older, and to have more family responsibilities (Coe & Elliott, 1999; Freddolino, 1998; Freddolino & Sutherland, 2000; Glezakos & Lee, 2001; Kleinpeter & Potts, 2000). I found that these demographic differences influence the reactions of the distance education students to course requirements. This was often reflected in students' attempts to negotiate the number of assigned readings, modify required course assignments, or change due dates. I also found that the distance education students tend to be more vocal and assertive in these attempts than the on-campus students. The predicament for me has been in attempting to find ways to satisfy student expectations without compromising academic standards.

Adaptation of one's teaching style. Instruction over interactive television is not always compatible with the Socratic approach to teaching that I had come to espouse and use in the more conventional classroom setting. The distance education students seem to prefer more how-to content rather than a teacher-student exchange that has greater potential for exploration of ideas and the development of critical and analytic thinking. As a result, I found myself acting as a dispenser of information and knowledge more often than I would prefer. One request, for instance, routinely made by my distance education students, is that I make available to them "model" term papers from previous students. The semester in which I accommodated this request, I discovered that individual student creativity was missing from the term papers. After I made up my mind to discontinue the practice, the next term's students expressed dissatisfaction. This difference in teacher-student expectations has the potential to affect how students evaluate their instructor.

Effects of travel. If an instructor is expected to visit each site in the distance education program, the geographic distance between the host campus and the distance education sites factors significantly into the time the instructor spends for each class. In my case, for instance, time spent on the road for site visits has varied from as little as 8 to 9 hours to as much as 3 days. Heavy ground traffic, plane delays, and airport inspections can take their toll. Any incentives, such as monetary compensation which I received, can help balance the effects of this challenge on the instructor.

Rewards

Notwithstanding the above challenges, I have found teaching in a distance education program to be rewarding, educational, and growth promoting in numerous ways.

More professionally trained social workers. A sustaining element in the midst of the many tribulations is my conviction that social work clients, independent of where they reside, have the right to service by competent social work practitioners. An outcome of professional education is competent practice. It is exhilarating to know that as an instructor in the distance education program, I am contributing to the supply of professionally trained and competent social workers in distant places.

Committed and highly motivated mature students. Many students in our urban on-campus program travel long distances and fight heavy traffic on congested freeways to get to their classes on time. Many of the students in the distance education program traveled even longer distances to attend class; some of them traveled from neighboring states. Weather conditions during the winter months made their travel difficult and hazardous, but they came. Their sense of commitment to their professional education and desire to become better and more competent social workers has had a powerful effect on me. Their numerous accounts of family hardships increased my sense of responsibility for providing quality education and effective teaching. I consciously worked to create a learning experience both inside and outside the classroom that would be sustaining for them and help increase or maintain their level of motivation. I tried to listen carefully and empathetically when my students engaged in negotiations about required assignments, readings, and due dates.

Opportunity to understand community-specific needs and resources. I have been pleased to have the opportunity to visit different sites and to spend time in new communities. Whenever possible, I walked through the streets, talked to residents, ate at local restaurants, and toured the host campuses. I found that my students are the best ambassadors for their towns. They have given me information about local places of interest, have walked around their campuses with me, dined with me, and invited me to their homes. I developed a deep appreciation of the unique strengths, social needs, and resources of the rural communities that I visited and in which my students will practice after graduation.

Diversity of rural communities. My students' papers have been a great source of information about client problems. At times I have been surprised to discover how different rural communities can be from each other in terms of problems and resources; I have seen how important it is to avoid generalizations about such communities. For instance, a rural community's ethnic composition, its proximity to an urban center, and the absence or availability of employment opportunities present the social work practitioner with different sets of challenges. What the students' papers, as well as other class assignments and class discussions, helped me understand better is that each rural community has its own character and its own needs for services. This realization has helped me to change some of my earlier conceptions of the American rural community and to make appropriate modifications to course content and assignments.

Invitation to address the graduates. During my long tenure as a university instructor, I have been presented with different forms of appreciation by students, both individually and collectively. Expressions of student appreciation have ranged from certificates of appreciation to plants, from a variety of items to be used in the office or items for more personal use to cards with well-worded sentiments. Only once, however, was I invited to be a speaker at a graduation ceremony, and the invitation came from the graduating class at the distance education site of California State University, Chico. I was pleasantly surprised and deeply honored. The students, with the help of their site coordinator, purchased my plane ticket and one student offered to accommodate me for the one night I needed to be in town since hotel accommodations were unavailable. I accepted, and following the university's commencement ceremonies, I addressed the MSW graduates at a small reception for their families and friends.

I congratulated the graduates for the successful completion of the educational journey on which they had embarked 3 years earlier and identified for them the privileges and responsibilities professional social workers have. I stressed the importance of professional and personal growth through continuing education and collaborative work, of ethical and competent practice. I made reference to the Code of Ethics of the National Association of Social Workers and reminded them of their responsibility to clients, to the agencies that will employ them, to the colleagues with whom they will network and collaborate, to the communities in which they will practice, to the profession into which they had gained membership.

Treat your clients with respect and dignity. . . . Use your power responsibly and judicially and never allow it to blind you to your ethical responsibility to serve and empower every client regardless

of their background and their behavior. . . . You have the knowledge and skill to assess the needs for new programs in the communities in which you will practice and you have the tools to advocate for the development of these programs. . . . Choose "the
road less traveled." The effort might be greater but the satisfaction
from the difference you will make will be deeper and personally
rewarding.

For me, receiving this invitation was a testament to the positive
impact that I had on this group of students as one of their distance education instructors. Delivering the keynote speech, having the opportunity to be among the students on the day they were awarded their
MSW degrees, and the privilege to meet the people who had supported them during 3 years of study were emotionally powerful experiences. The time that I had spent on the road flying to their distant
site during my three-year association with their program became an
insignificant issue on graduation day.

The great teachers who planted the seed in my mind that one day
I too could become an effective teacher are forever present in my en-
counters as a classroom instructor. I learned much from these earlier
teachers; I have, as well, learned much from my students—both those
that I have encountered on campus and those that I worked with
from a distance. The learning from the latter group has been unique
and effusive.

REFERENCES

Coe, J. R., & Elliott, d. (1999). An evaluation of teaching direct practice
    courses in a distance education program for rural settings. *Journal of So-
    cial Work Education, 35*(3), 353–366.
Faria, G., & Perry-Burney, G. (2002). A technology-based MSW program.
    Journal of Teaching in Social Work, 22(3/4), 155–169.
Foster, M., & Rehner, T. (1998). Part-time MSW distance education: A pro-
    gram evaluation. *Computers in Human Services, 15*(2/3), 9–21.
Freddolino, P. P. (2002). Thinking "outside the box" in social work distance
    education: Not just for distance anymore. *Electronic Journal of Social
    Work, 1*(1). Retrieved September 22, 2003. http://www.ajsw.net/issue/
    vol1/num1/article6.pdf
Freddolino, P. P. (1998). Building on experience: Lessons from a distance edu-
    cation M.S.W. program. *Computers in Human Services, 15*(2/3), 39–50.
Freddolino, P. P., & Sutherland, C. A. (2000). Assessing the comparability of
    classroom environments in graduate social work education delivered

via interactive instructional television. *Journal of Social Work Education, 36*(1), 115–129.

Glezakos, A., & Lee, C. D. (2001). Distance and on-campus MSW students: How they perform and what they tell us. *Professional Development: The International Journal of Continuing Social Work Education, 4*(2), 54–61.

Heitkamp, T. (2000). A decade of lessons learned in delivering a social work distance education program. *Arete, 24*(1), 48–54.

Huff, M. T. (2000). A comparison study of live instruction versus interactive television for teaching MSW students critical thinking skills. *Research on Social Work Practice, 10*(4), 400–416.

Kleinpeter, C., & Potts, M. K. (2000). Distance education: Teaching practice methods using interactive television. *Professional Development: The International Journal of Continuing Social Work Education, 3*(3), 37–43.

Lowell, J. R. (1946). Emerson the lecturer. In H. Peterson (Ed.), *Great teachers* (pp. 331–340). New York: Vintage Books.

Mill, S. J. (1946). Unwasted years. In H. Peterson (Ed.), *Great teachers* (pp. 15–42). New York: Vintage Books.

Patchner, M. A., Petracchi, H. E., & Wise, S. (1998). Outcomes of ITV and face-to-face instruction in a social work research methods course. *Computers in Human Services, 15*(2/3), 23–38.

Petracchi, H. E., & Patchner, M. A. (2000). Social work students and their learning environment: A comparison of interactive television, face-to-face instruction, and the traditional classroom. *Journal of Social Work Education, 36*(2), 225–346.

Petracchi, H. E., & Patchner, M. E. (2001). A comparison of live instruction and interactive televised teaching: A 2-year assessment of teaching an MSW research methods course. *Research on Social Work Practice, 11*(1), 108–117.

Pullias, E. V., & Lockhart, A. (1963). *Toward excellence in college teaching.* Dubuque, IA: W. C. Brown.

Resnick, H., & Anderson, P. S. (2002). Conclusion. *Journal of Technology in Human Services, 20*(2/3), 369–371.

Sheafor, B. W. (1996). Taking the mountain to Mohammed: Enhancing rural human services through distance education. *Journal of Baccalaureate Social Work, 1*(2), 27–39.

Chapter **6**

CONNECTING WITH STUDENTS

Paul Abels

SEEING AND BEING SEEN

What makes teaching in distance education unique? The usual responses include the use of technology, both how it limits and expands what the teacher and students can do. Then there are the factors related to vast geographic distances and cultural differences, that it minimizes face-to-face interaction with the students, and that certain traditional tools used in the classroom may differ—such as larger print on overheads, or in my case, not being able to stand and pace while teaching. I am sure anyone who has taught in both DE and traditional classes has other contrasts they might make. Certainly there are educational concepts that are universal, neither bound to the traditional classroom nor to distance education. But I believe there is another factor, rarely if ever mentioned, that I believe marks a major difference in distance education that needs to be addressed, and may have relevance for the puzzle I faced with one of my DE classes.

I believe an important factor about the difference in DE and traditional teaching that we have taken for granted, perhaps because it is more of a psychological factor, relates to the way people react to seeing and being seen. "Seeing comes before words. The child looks and recognizes before it can speak" (Berger, 1972, p. 7). A person may pay more attention to what they see than to what they hear. Why do I feel different when I teach a regular class than I do teaching in a DE class? A common experience in interactive distance education is that students see each other on television, and they know they are being seen. The teacher is seen on television and knows he or she is being seen. How does the way we see things and think about being seen influence the teaching/learning situation? (Norton, 2002) Though students in the traditional classroom may wonder about who the other students might be, their concern about how they might be seen by the other students may be important, but is not a major consideration. The instructor might wonder if the class will be a "good" one, yet there is little concern about how he or she will appear to them as far as physical appearance goes, though instructors are certainly concerned about their appearance of competence. I believe those factors are different when ITV enters the picture. Now this is just a theory, and I often tell my students to be careful of theories ("There is nothing as bad as a good theory") because it often limits their view, but it is important to explore this further.

Some faculty in DE classes play back their sessions, viewing themselves and the students. Is it to improve their teaching or is it to see how they appear? In discussions with some of the faculty, they often speak about having a good class, pointing out on the video not what the class did, but what they did.

The nature of television requires performers and viewers, and in the case of DE the major performer—in this case the instructor—takes on a persona that needs to be maintained throughout the course. Although this may seem strange to the reader at first, remember that we are dealing with students who have grown up with television, watching a dramatic or comedy series episode after episode. The characters, the performers, can be relied on to play their parts throughout the series. In social work we translate these expected patterns of worker behavior into social concepts such as role theory, or helping contracts. In the television age and milieu of DE, teachers are expected to stay in character. They are being viewed in that way. In traditional teaching the students are in a classroom. In DE the students are in a theater: they watch, but they are also being watched by the teacher and by others.

This leads to another related point on the differences in the DE classroom. Foucault talked about the power of the "gaze," the ability to control behavior by making people believe their actions are under constant observation. This ability to observe continually has historic roots in the areas of discipline and control and may psychologically impact the nature of the classroom-learning situation (Foucault, 1995). Comparing DE with real television may carry the metaphor a bit far, but to deny that television has influenced our perceptions and actions in the past few decades is to ignore data on the importance of the TV media as a marketing mechanism. I suggest that distance education when presented through ITV becomes a situation in which both parties are under constant observation. One faculty person even commented that she could have the cameras focus on the small group discussions, listening to each of the groups as they work. And of course all of the other groups can view the same scene or be seen in turn and listen in on the conversations.

How does the above relate to the title of this chapter, to my puzzle about connections? Remember, I am talking about a theory, a hunch I have about the relationship. The readers will have to make their own judgments related to my brief theoretical reflections. This chapter discusses an experience in which I, as an instructor in a DE class, had my vision of how I wanted to be seen; at first that vision was supported, then it was shattered. My connections (in TV that might be called ratings) with the students, strong at first, began to decline near the end of the semester. In an effort to understand what might have led to this unanticipated outcome, I believe it would be important to put my approach to teaching with this class in context. I will attempt this by looking briefly at my teaching approach in general and then at my connections with this particular DE class.

Teaching is a very personal experience, both for the teacher and for the student. Instructors develop their philosophy and styles of teaching based on frames of reference or worldview of what is true, and they have their own ideas of what they may believe are important to achieve with students. For social work educators, I assume that however different their views might be, they recognize the importance of connecting, of building a learning relationship with the class as important, at least to some degree. In addition, they would agree that their prime task is successfully accomplishing the delivery of the course content and purpose to the students. In a sense, establishing connections with the students is a tool for that accomplishment. Often the clue to the success of the teacher-learner transaction is related to presenting the content in a context that the students can feel is real and provides a personal connection with the material. We are faced with a parallel process of connecting with the students at the same time we are helping them connect with the material.

Just as we have come to realize the importance of relationship in any helping situation, we have come to understand that the relationship between teacher and student is an important one. It is important for me to get across to the students that there is a reciprocal relationship between us: I can't be a teacher without a class, and they can't become the professionals they want to be without the classes and the teachers that come with them. We need each other.

Talking about our mutual responsibilities in the teaching-learning transaction is one way to start the relationship, but there must be a feeling of mutuality about values; and there must be a feeling of trust, which takes time and is often subverted by the students' own experience with authority figures; and in the class there must be a sense that history is an ongoing reality.

I usually ask all my students if there is anyone in the class who has never been embarrassed or put down by a teacher, from kindergarten to their most recent educational experiences. They are told they will not have to talk of the experience, just a show of hands. Not one student has ever raised a hand. As they look around the class, they are as amazed as I used to be when I first started to ask that question. I continue by asking what this means for their involvement as a learner. They speak of the resistance to trust faculty, a reluctance to speak up in class, and a wish not to contradict the teacher. A few students say it has not deterred them in any way, but from time to time they recall the incident and feel themselves blushing. I apologize for bringing these buried thoughts to mind, and add that the question I asked of them brings back memories to me as well. Certain situations in the classroom bring out strong emotional feelings, and the instructor needs to be aware of these and of the ethical implications. The matter of emotional concerns in a classroom has been of increasing interest in the DE field (Mason, 2002).

The discussion that follows is almost always open—we don't discuss the content of the event, but rather their feelings about it—and the discussion soon moves from their experiences to their work with clients' and/or staff's feelings as the classes' purpose demands, and then to the nature of the helping relationship. How might a client feel? How might a worker feel if embarrassed by an administrator? How might they behave in the future after such experiences? The subject of control by those in authority becomes a central topic in these discussions, as well as their sense of powerlessness. They would not want to work in such a situation. They would not want to be a student in that type of class.

CONNECTING IN DISTANCE EDUCATION IS DIFFERENT

Connecting positively with students is important, and one of the concerns I had with my DE class was how to enhance that connection. For a start I asked them not to change seats and to have name cards in front of them so I could get to know them and identify them by name (try pointing to a person on a TV screen). In addition, in the more traditional classroom setting, some students will come up to you after class to make a comment or ask a question, so I announced to the DE classes that I would remain on the TV for 20 minutes after class if any of them wanted to talk to me. They had to realize that other students would also hear the question and the response. I added that private questions could be e-mailed and I would answer by the next day, two at the most. They had used e-mail and the Web previously and I knew that would be available, but they were very pleased and surprised that I would stay late on the TV to talk to them.

It has been my experience that there are courses that are preferred by students, and courses that they might prefer not to take if they had a choice. Certainly in the preferred category are the practice courses and fieldwork. Without trying to rank those not on the top, I think I have a fairly reasonable idea of what to expect when I teach certain courses. I was particularly concerned with the required administration course, as it was my first DE experience. I had taught it about five times in our regular program and knew that students would rather have had a more clinically oriented course. I anticipated the worst and decided to start by connecting them to the course and their teacher at the same time.

After 40 years of teaching it was a very new approach for me. As a way of introducing myself and the course, I went through my social-work life from camp counselor, practitioner, administrator educator to the current class, relating about a dozen changes in the landscape to show how administration or administrators impacted my life at each stage. As we moved through that first half-hour, I could feel the puzzlement, and than the concentration. The connections with the class as reported by the students and the liaison's unsolicited e-mails that evening was a very positive and uplifting one. In a sense, the connections were enhanced because I violated their expectations not only by my transparency, but by making administration a vital, live part of social work.

I had always worked hard to connect with students, and often used the group dynamics that a classroom allows to have the students help each other and be responsible for some of the direction of the class. This may be a carryover from my group social-work experience and belief in mutual aid and support groups. In fact, I found that there was a great deal of mutual aid and support taking place in the DE classes, and more of a "we" feeling, perhaps because it was a new experience, perhaps because they felt like outsiders research project.

CONNECTING THROUGH THE USE OF A LOG

In each of my classes I require that the students keep a log; they are asked to note and reflect on items related to the specific course connections with field practice and general social-work material related to their current experiences. These are handed in three times during the courses, the first a few weeks into the course so I can see if they are clear about my expectations. I respond to many of the items they write about, some of which are personal revelations motivated by reading of a similar situation, or a strong reaction to a horror story like the death of child through neglect. At times the students will e-mail me after my response with some reaction. I see this interaction as a valuable learning tool for the student and also a major way of establishing mutual connections.

Relevant items come from the media or from personal experience of major import. This was certainly the case with some of the entries in their logs related to 9/11. Some of the verbatim entries from more than 100 that dealt with the students' reactions can be found in an issue published by *Reflections* (Summer 2002) that dealt with the horrific 9/11 tragedy.

Most spoke of their fears and anxiety, of "staying glued to the radio" or of their inability to concentrate, of the horrors they saw, attempts to reach relatives or friends back East, their fear for the future. Others spoke of their children and the impact of the violence they had seen A few mentioned their work with teens, who were usually very cool but now were visibly upset. A few mentioned their agencies, how shocked the staff looked, and that many of their clients did not show up. But for the most part they spoke of their own feelings, the terror and the thoughts for the future.

A few noted that their agency made no mention of the 9/11 attack during or after the event, and they were surprised and disappointed. Staff in one agency set up their own meetings to help each other. (At a later time this became an area of discussion in the administration class).

This summary hardly reflects the anguished voices of the students and while the specific items were not discussed in class we did discuss 9/11 at the next class session. Interestingly, the discussion did not have the power of the log entries. It is interesting how much comes out when people start to write about their experiences and their feelings. The discussion did serve the purpose of helping the students make connections with each other and in some cases with the instructor. It was an ability to share feelings with others, but also a sense of us all being able to count on each other. Unlike other classroom discussions, no one interrupted others' comments, nor did I. I was no more an expert on feelings and solutions than they were. We were all in the same boat. The landscape had changed for all of us, and I need to thank them for their willingness to share their thoughts and the help we all obtained from the discussions.

A PUZZLE

At the end of the semester students are given an evaluation form to fill out (the same one used for all the students at the university). Because each DE course was given to two classes at the same time, one might assume there would be little but not too much difference in their perceptions of my work with them. That held true in all my DE classes except one; thus, the puzzle.

When I was a social work student, I recall my research professor saying that whenever you do research and find that one of your samples differs a great deal from the others, try to find out or understand how that difference could be accounted for. Why for example would one class judge the assignments less appropriate than another class? Why would one class see me as less prepared than the other? What was the difference that caused the difference?

Here's what I think: With one of the classes (let's call them Alpha), I violated an unwritten contract. It is customary procedure for the faculty person to make two visits to the distant site over a weekend, once at the start of the semester and again near the end of the semester. The class is then broadcast to the other site from the community being visited. The visits are an opportunity for the faculty to get to know the students a little more closely. Usually there is a potluck supper at one of the student's homes. On one occasion the students had been told I sang folk songs, and they brought a guitar to the potluck. I sang of course; as a guest it was an expectation I could not ignore.

These visits seemed to have a great deal of importance to the students; they wanted to get to know the instructors in a more personal way. They wanted to ask the type of questions they might not feel comfortable asking in the classroom. A simple question like, How did you become interested in social work? Or a more complex question such as, How do we compare with the students in your regular classes? On one occasion when I brought my wife with me, they insisted on taking us for a tour of the city, to the museums, the art studios, and seemed to want us to see the context of their lives.

Well, to make a longer story short, I did not carry out my second visit to Alpha as we had to change the visit date due to some type of mix-up. Although I explained the circumstances to them at the prior session, and again during my 20-minute after-class conversation with them, it was clear they were disappointed.

Of course, there were difference in the makeup of the class. But the non-visit was the only event that was different between the two classes, and I believe it may have led to the difference in the final class evaluation. Now the way our evaluation is counted, three or four students listing a few questions low can illuminate the difference, so it was not that the entire class rated me lower, but a few did. Although it may be that they didn't learn, or didn't like my teaching style, I think it was a more intense response. I believe the students might have felt I violated my commitment, or they might have felt I had a preference for the other class on view at the same time.

Did I do what I had hoped I never would do, embarrass or put down students? Is that what the problem was? Was it an illustration of violating the importance of social capital, the connections requiring mutual values and trust and reciprocity? Was it about the "civics" of the teaching-learning situation? (Sirianni & Friedland, 1995), and had I violated the civics? That was one of my first conclusions, yet it seemed too easy an assumption to make, so were there other factors at work?

I may have also violated their expectations by stepping out of the character we had both created over time on the TV. That may be one of the problems with DE. In the traditional class it would have been easier for them to discuss their concerns about the visit with me, we might have worked out alternatives, had pizza together, something more special at the last class. That was not an alternative on DE in this particular situation. One class was watching and listening to the other. I believe there was mixture of many factors at work. I will need to try to unravel the Gordian knot. That's what is so exciting about teaching; there is so much to learn, both on and off of TV.

REFERENCES

Berger, J. (1972), *Ways of seeing*. London: Penquin Books.

Foucault, M. (1995). *Discipline & punish: The birth of the prison*. NY: Vintage Press.

Mason, A. (2002). The emotional commotion. *Interactions: New Visions of Human Computer Interaction, 10*(6), 29–33.

Norton, D. (2002). Does it matter what technology users see first? *Interactions: New Visions of Human Computer Interaction, 10*(2), 9–12.

Sirianni, C., & Friedland, L. (1995). *Social capital and civic innovation; Learning and capacity building from the 1960s to the 1990s*. Paper presented at the American Sociological Association Annual Meeting, August 20, 1995, Washington, DC.

PART 4

Research in Distance Education

Chapter 7

MEASURING THE DISTANCE: EVALUATION OF DISTANCE EDUCATION IN SOCIAL WORK

Marilyn K. Potts

This chapter provides an overview of the current state of distance education (DE) evaluation efforts in social work. Systems theory is used as a framework, a model for integrating the current literature and informing future research. Recommendations for moving beyond comparability analyses, based primarily on student satisfaction and grades, are then presented. Although most of the DE courses and programs discussed use various interactive television (ITV) technologies, the principles are applicable to online coursework.

Education in general is into its third generation of DE, beginning with a generation of correspondence courses since the 1890s, evolving to a second generation of radio and ITV communication, and then to a third generation of online coursework. Although social work appears to skip the first generation, various DE programs in the discipline—primarily one-way or two-way audio and/or video—have grown exponentially during the past 20 years. Our own second generation, Web-based or Web-enhanced courses, currently shows a similar level of growth.

FACTORS DRIVING DISTANCE EDUCATION EVALUATION

It is perhaps only a small exaggeration to claim that DE programs are the most extensively evaluated educational endeavors in our discipline. This is attributable to three factors: (a) increased accountability for student learning outcomes, (b) Council on Social Work Education (CSWE) requirements for documentation of comparability between DE and traditional programs, and (c) the emergence of venues for dissemination of DE evaluation results.

Increased Accountability for Student Learning Outcomes

Most social work DE programs are relatively new, emerging during a time of increased accountability for student learning outcomes. CSWE always required documentation of program quality for accreditation but recently altered its focus. According to previous Educational Policy and Accreditation Standards (EPAS), outcomes must be measured and the results of program evaluations must be used. Evaluative Standards 1.4 and 1.5 stated the following:

> 1.4—The program must specify the outcome measures and measurement procedures that are to be used systematically in evaluating the program, and that will enable it to determine its success in achieving its desired objectives.
> 1.5—The program must show evidence that it engages in ongoing, systematic self-study and evaluation of its total program, and show evidence that the results of evaluation affect program planning and curriculum design. (Council on Social Work Education [CSWE], 1994)

Emphasis on accountability culminated in more specific directions evaluating each program outcome. The revised EPAS, in force June 2002, indicate that general program evaluations are unacceptable. No longer is there reference to the "total program"; the current evaluation plan must focus on each specific program objective. Evaluative Standards 8.0 and 8.1 now state as follows:

> 8.0—The program has an assessment plan and procedures for evaluating the outcome of each program objective. The plan specifies the measurement procedures and methods used to evaluate the outcome of each objective.
> 8.1—The program implements its plan to evaluate the outcome of

each program objective and shows evidence that the analysis is used continuously to affirm and improve the educational program. (CSWE, 2001)

Comparability of Alternative Programs

Second, and specifically related to DE program evaluation, is the CSWE requirement that all alternative programs establish comparability with traditional modes of delivery programs. EPAS in effect during the initiation of most DE programs defined "alternative programs" as involving change in one or more components of a program already accredited. Those alternative programs involving substantive change, such as off-campus arrangements or differences in geographic location, required CSWE approval before program implementation. In particular DE programs were mentioned under Evaluative Standard 7.1 and their evaluation requirements under Evaluative Standard 7.3. Note the following emphasis on "equal quality . . . relative to its standard program." This requirement was a primary driving force behind the emphasis on comparability analyses in the current literature on DE evaluation.

> 7.1—An alternative program that offers the equivalent of one or more academic years of the social work degree program, whether the class or field curriculum or both, in an off-campus location must submit a proposal to the Commission on Accreditation for approval before implementing the program.
> 7.3—The alternative program proposal must include a detailed plan that presents the rationale and goals of the program and elaborates on the curriculum content and objectives. The program is to document the equal quality of its alternative program relative to its standard program. (CSWE, 1994)

The emphasis on comparability analyses continues under the new EPAS. Again, off-campus programs are specifically noted under "Program Changes and Alternative Programs" and are required to document the same level of quality offered by the traditional program.

> Over time, in addition to offering a traditional full-time social work education program, a program may wish to make changes to its structure, for example, by adding an off-campus program, offering a joint degree, a part-time version of the accredited program, or distance education courses. Program changes are not separately ac-

credited and therefore fall under the accreditation of the baccalaureate or master's program of which they are a part. Consequently, it is expected that these changes, including alternative programs, offer the same level of quality offered by the full-time accredited program. This fact is reflected in the program's self-study documentation. (CSWE, 2003)

Further, off-campus and entire DE programs are among the types of changes requiring prior notification before implementation.

> Notification of the Commission is required in writing when programs make significant changes while remaining in compliance with all standards. Examples include changes in the structure of the accredited program, such as adding a dual-degree program or offering an off-campus program, a new part-time program, or an entire distance education program. . . . An educational specialist reviews the documentation, may seek clarifying information, and reports the notification to the Commission. (CSWE, 2003)

Venues for Dissemination

Third, several venues for presentation and publication of DE evaluation results have emerged. Presentation opportunities include the annual Technology Conference sponsored by the University of South Carolina from 1997 to 2001 and the Distance Education Symposia within CSWE's Annual Program Meeting (these activities will be held co–currently in 2004). Technology Conference proceedings are typically available on CD-ROM and are published in the *Journal of Technology in Human Services*. Additional publication opportunities include complete issues on DE evaluation by *Research in Social Work Practice* and the *Journal of Technology in Human Services*, as well as special sections on DE and technology in the *Journal of Social Work Education*. Researchers engaged in the comparability analyses described above thus found ample opportunities to disseminate their findings. In addition, largely because of their attendance at the above conferences, a small but cohesive cadre of DE leaders emerged to stimulate each other's thinking, contemplate the state of the art of DE evaluation, and make recommendations for filling gaps in our knowledge base. Many ideas for further research suggested are derived from conversations among members of the Distance Education Research Group (DERG) of CSWE's Annual Program Meeting.

COMPARABILITY OF DISTANCE EDUCATION AND TRADITIONAL PROGRAMS

Is the medium the message? Does dining in or dining out affect the nutritional value of the food we eat? Although arguable, given the diversity of student learning styles and the diversity of types of courses taught in social work curricula, DE advocates would say no to both questions, maintaining instead that DE in social work has established its comparability with traditional modes of delivery. Owing largely to the aforementioned reasons for the proliferation of the DE evaluation literature, many studies exist documenting the equivalence or superiority of DE programs in terms of student satisfaction (based on ratings of instructional quality) and outcomes (based on self-perceived learning and grades).

Student Satisfaction

Results from DE student evaluations suggest that satisfaction levels with instructional quality are at least equivalent to those obtained for traditional courses (Coe & Elliott, 1999; Coe & Gandy, 1998; Dalton, 2001; Haga & Heitkamp, 2000; Heitkamp, 1995; Jennings, Siegel, & Conklin, 1995; Kelley, 1993; & Sorensen, 1997; Kleinpeter & Potts, 2000; Kikuchi Potts & Hagan, 2000; Potts & Kleinpeter, 2003). Similarly, Freddolino and Sutherland (2000) found that DE students in one off-campus location had higher overall scores on an Adult Classroom Environment Scale than did on-campus students taking the same four courses in a traditional "non-linked" classroom.

Our own research on a DE program using ITV showed moderate to high ratings (3.2 to 4.8 on a 1 to 5 point scale) for overall DE program quality, which was comparable to ratings given by on-campus students (Potts & Hagan, 2000; Potts & Kleinpeter, 2003). Satisfaction with the technology among DE students alone was also moderate to high (3.0 to 4.4 on a 1 to 5 point scale). Scores rose and fell within three cohorts of students and across 8 years (thus far) of evaluation, corresponding with technological glitches such as the need for a new amplifier at one site, audio static created by placing a microphone next to an air conditioning unit at another site, video fragmentation suggesting to students that they were experiencing LSD flashbacks, and the occasional total system breakdown (which we never fully understood but which was fixed by technology experts from the system). Nevertheless, learning occurred (see section below on outcomes) and qualitative expressions of frustration were tempered by the realization that the program was valuable because of its content and the lack of viable educational alternatives. Students stated: "Although the technology is not perfect, the transmission of knowledge takes place." "Technology is very frustrating; however, our guest speakers have been excellent and this would not have been available if not for the technology." "We may have a few problems, but we know that we are pioneers in this use of technology."

Others have noted somewhat mixed results regarding student satisfaction. Although Ligon, Markward, and Yegidis (1997) found that a substance abuse course taught in a DE format received higher ratings than the same course taught in a traditional format, the opposite results were noted for a family practice course. Another evaluation of two practice courses, both taught by alternating in-person and ITV instruction, found no significant differences in student appraisals for one course, while students exposed to both methods preferred in-person instruction for the other course (Thyer, Artelt, Markward, & Dozier, 1998).

Satisfaction ratings, while valuable, do not address learning outcomes. In addition, most satisfaction comparisons between DE and traditional students are based on courses taught by different instructors. This is less true for single course evaluations, which can feasibly involve one instructor assigned to teach both in DE and traditional classrooms, but overall program evaluations cannot claim that the instructors assigned to teach DE courses are the same individuals as those assigned to teach concurrently offered on-campus courses.

Student Outcomes

Empirical data also show that the educational achievements of DE students are at least comparable to those of traditional students. Compared to on-campus cohorts, DE students appear to earn equivalent grades (Coe & Elliott, 1999; Forster & Rehner, 1998; Haagenstad & Kraft, 1998; Haga & Heitkamp, 1995; Hollister & McGee, 1998; Kleinpeter & Potts, 2000; Patchner, Petracchi, & Wise, 1997; Petracchi & Patchner, 2001a, 2000b; Potts & Hagan, 2000; Potts & Kleinpeter, 2003; Raymond, 1988; Sheafor, 1994). Petracchi and Morgenbesser (1994) found that a filmed version of an elective course resulted in higher grades than an in-person version of the same course. Our own work has shown that multicultural sensitivity scale scores increased significantly over the course of an MSW program among DE students, while no difference was apparent among on-campus students in the same program model (Potts & Hagan, 2000).

Although course grades provide some evidence of learning, actual practice skills are harder to measure. Self-reported skills are suspect due to social desirability biases and the phenomenon of "not knowing what we don't know." Third-party assessments of practice skills, typically from field instructors, are scarce in the DE literature. We found that field instructor ratings for DE and on-campus students were either identical or similar (Kleinpeter & Potts, 2000; Potts & Hagan, 2000; Potts & Kleinpeter, 2003).

Yet, as noted above regarding the satisfaction literature, the outcomes literature, whether based on grades, attitudes, values, self-reported skills, or third-party assessments, is generally plagued by questions concerning the comparability of instructors in DE and traditional courses.

Alumni Outcomes

A logical extension of the emphasis on comparability between DE and traditional students is to turn to similar evaluations based on DE and traditional alumni (Hollister & Kim, 2001, 2003; Potts & Kleinpeter, 2001). This is especially important given the rationale for many DE programs, that is, the need to increase the availability of professional social workers in underserved communities. Do DE alumni remain in their communities? Do they advance professionally to supervisory or administrative positions? Do their responsibilities increase? Do their salaries increase?

Hollister and Kim (2003) compared DE and on-campus alumni on perceptions of the adequacy of program supports and self-perceived competencies. DE alumni consisted of two groups: those exposed to full ITV instruction (six or more courses) and those exposed to partial ITV instruction (at least one but less than six courses). Six of seven aspects of program support showed comparability, while full ITV alumni were less satisfied with the adequacy of library resources. Of 20 self-perceived competencies, 16 showed comparability, while the remaining four were rated significantly higher by full ITV alumni.

Our own evaluation of DE and on-campus alumni in the same year and program model showed that DE alumni had higher levels of satisfaction with faculty, but lower levels of satisfaction with administration (Potts & Kleinpeter, 2001). Using the same self-perceived competencies instrument as Hollister and Kim (2003), we found no differences between DE and on-campus alumni for 17 of 20 items. However, DE alumni had higher ratings regarding the extent to which the program enhanced their understanding of social services policies and practices and their ability to conduct research, but lower ratings regarding the extent to which the program had enhanced their ability to use computers.

We made a beginning attempt to study the extent to which DE alumni showed evidence of professional socialization, an elusive concept that many talk about, particularly critics of DE (Kreuger & Stretch, 1997, 2000), but few can define or measure. Membership in NASW was identical for DE and on-campus alumni (39%). DE and on-campus alumni were similar in terms of involvement in volunteer work and presentations at professional conferences. More on-campus alumni had published an article or chapter, while more DE alumni received a grant for research or training. Slightly more on-campus alumni joined our alumni association, but more than 3 times as many DE alumni attended an alumni function.

Perhaps disappointingly, only 21% of our DE alumni received a promotion, 29% received a pay raise, and 33% reported increased job responsibilities. However, these reports were nearly identical to those among our on-campus alumni (21%, 33%, and 29%, respectively). Less disappointingly, nearly all DE alumni reported finding employment prior to or immediately after graduation. Nearly three fourths experienced a job search lasting zero months, probably because they were hired by their pre-MSW employer or internship agency. Consistent with our program's emphasis on public social services, nearly three fourths of DE alumni (compared to only half of on-campus alumni) held jobs in the public sector. Although DE alumni salaries were lower than those of on-campus alumni, this is probably attributable to differences in rural and urban costs of living and thus salary standards.

Impact on Larger Community

Anecdotal evidence suggests that DE programs make a difference in their communities. Agency staff has been heard to state that they have benefited both directly and vicariously because of the presence of interns. Many professors from the host institution provide in-service training and continuing education programs during their visits to DE sites. McFall and Freddolino (1998, 2000a), in their survey of agencies providing DE field instruction, found that the presence of interns allowed these agencies to provide more services, enhanced access to new knowledge about interventions, and exposed them to new uses of technology. On the other hand, questions have been raised about certain negative effects, such as the time required for adequate supervision, complications due to student scheduling, threats to client confidentiality, and concern over the sharing of proprietary information. One might add the increased paperwork involved in evaluating interns to this list, as well as the time required for faculty field liaison visits. However, no evidence suggests that these concerns are unique to DE.

CATEGORIZATION OF DISTANCE EDUCATION RESEARCH: APPLES AND ORANGES AND PLUMS

There are many ways to cut the pie in classifying DE evaluations. One categorization scheme comes from any basic research methods textbook: implementation, formative versus summative, process versus outcome, impact, comparative, and so forth. As suggested earlier, the emphasis has been on formative/process (satisfaction), summative/ outcome (grades and changes in values, attitudes, and skills), and comparative studies, while cost-benefit and cost-effectiveness studies are lacking. Implementation reports are anecdotal in nature and little is known about longer-term impacts.

Based on Moore's widely used typology of the types of interactions required in DE education, evaluations may be classified as involving learner-content interaction (e.g., grades and changes in values, attitudes, and skills), learner-instructor interaction (e.g., satisfaction with instructional quality), and learner-learner interaction (Moore, 1989; Moore & Kearsley, 1996). Much is known about the first two types of interactions, while less is known about the third. An exception is Rooney, Izaksonas, and Macy's (1998) report of within-site cohesion and between-site conflict. Others (Hillman, Willis, & Gunawardena, 1994) have presented a fourth type of interaction, that of learner-technology. Though DE evaluation reports may mention the type of technology used, no systematic comparison has been made of the effects of various modes of delivery.

In a thorough review by Macy, Rooney, Hollister, and Freddolino (2001), the DE evaluation literature was divided (as was done here) according to whether the content concerned student satisfaction or learning outcomes or both. These authors divided the existing literature according to whether the evaluation had been based on a single course or an overall degree program, noting a preponderance of the former and a scarcity of the latter. Individual courses included social policy, substance abuse, research methods, statistics, child welfare, human behavior and the social environment, human diversity, social welfare history, social welfare law, practice methods, and field instruction.

Variations in research methodology should be noted. First, sampling: Most evaluations focused on students or faculty evaluations of students or both, while far fewer focused on alumni (Haga & Heitkamp, 2000; Hollister & Kim, 2001, 2003; Macy, 1999; Potts & Kleinpeter, 2001), although it is recognized that many DE programs are too new to have a large cadre of alumni. Little is known about faculty satisfaction, faculty concerns, and the appropriate reward structure for teaching in DE programs (Litzelfelner, Wiehe, & Olson, 2001) or about the views of agency staff and other professionals in DE communities (McFall & Freddolino, 2000b). What is known about the views of clients in these communities comes indirectly from field instructor evaluations of student-client interactions and outcomes.

Second, instrumentation: Most evaluations rely on self-administered surveys and/or existing data on grades and other assessments of student performance, such as critical thinking skills (Huff, 2000). Following trends in social work education overall, focus groups and portfolios are other recommended options (Mehrotra, Hollister, & McGahey, 2001), along with a greater emphasis on qualitative methods.

Third, design issues: Some DE evaluations include a comparison group, while others do not, relying instead on one-group pre/post testing at best. An exception is the work of Dalton (2001), which included a comparison group taught by the same instructor, pre/post testing, and follow-up testing.

Given these and other differences, the literature on DE education lacks coherence. DE programs are consistently described as involving the separation of teacher and learner during at least a majority of the instructional process, the use of educational media to carry course content, and the provision of communication between teacher and learner (Verduin & Clark, 1991). Yet, DE programs vary widely in each of these respects. In teacher-learner separation, the number of in-person sessions per course may range from none to several. Overall curricula may include some courses taught entirely through DE technology, some courses taught partly through DE technology and partly by on-campus faculty traveling to DE sites, and some courses taught face-to-face by local faculty. Some DE programs require a period of residency at the host campus. Programs also vary whether, and to the extent that local site coordinators are involved in instructional activities. In use of educational media, the delivery system may involve audio and video interaction, supplemented or not supplemented by online materials. In teacher-learner communication, interaction may be one-way or two-way, synchronous or nonsynchronous. In-class interaction may be supplemented or not supplemented by e-mail contact, discussion boards, chat rooms, and other forums. So many variations exist that the independent variables in DE evaluation as a whole are a mixture of apples and oranges and plums.

SYSTEMS THEORY: A FRAMEWORK FOR COHERENCE

Systems theory provides a framework for integrating these disparate factors (Moore & Kearsley, 1996). Beginning with the work of biologist Ludwig von Bertalanffy (1968), systems theory influenced several social work practice approaches, such as the ecosystems, biopsychosocial, and person-in-environment models (Anderson & Carter, 1990). A social system consists of interacting and interdependent persons, such as DE participants. Systems boundaries may be permeable (as in the case of open systems), but there is more interchange among components within the system, such as a DE classroom, than between the system and components outside its boundaries. Open systems continuously exchange energy, in the form of information and other resources, with their environment. Input refers to energy imported from the environment, throughput refers to the process by which the system acts upon this energy, and output refers to the product exported into the environment.

Systems may contain subsystems and may be contained by suprasystems. What is viewed as a system, subsystem, or suprasystem depends on the primary focus of attention, but each level is interwoven with all other levels. A DE classroom may be viewed as a system while also being viewed as part of a suprasystem—that of the social work program—which in turn is part of a larger suprasystem, the university. A DE classroom may be viewed as consisting of several subsystems, such as instructor-student dyads, student-student dyads, and larger student groups. The community in which the DE program is located is another type of suprasystem (Potts & Hagan, 2000).

Input

Input includes various factors relevant to the need for, and design of, a DE program. Some stem from the local community, such as the dearth of MSW social workers in many rural areas. Others stem from the technological infrastructure available to the program, the host institution's resources, the host institution's curricular emphasis, CSWE curriculum standards, and the availability of outside funding. Background characteristics of the students themselves should also be viewed as relevant input factors.

   Empirical data are lacking regarding these input factors and their effects, with the exception of background characteristics of students. In order to examine baseline equivalence between DE and on-campus students, most of the comparability analyses described above include a comparison of demographics. Thus, we know that DE students tend to be older and have more social work experience than their on-campus counterparts. Gender ratios are typically similar (with a preponderance of women). The results of ethnicity comparisons vary widely, with some DE programs, particularly those in rural areas, consisting mostly of non-Hispanic Whites and others actually being more diverse than their host institution. In our own experience, several of our DE sites contained a higher proportion of Native Americans and Hispanics than is the case among on-campus students (Potts & Hagan, 2000; Potts & Kleinpeter, 2003). The following are questions for further research involving input factors.

1. What institutional infrastructures contribute to the success of DE programs? These include administrative structures, such as the existence of positions for a DE coordinator and local site coordinators, their job descriptions, their location within the institutional hierarchy, and their opportunities for interaction with on-campus faculty (Hagan & Potts, 1999). They also include interactions between the host institution and the local community. Do DE programs need to be attached to local universities? How are local faculty and social services providers involved in planning and teaching? What types of interinstitutional arrangements exist?

2. What technologies are available from the host institution? Who controls them? Who staffs them? Who pays for them? If technological support is not available through the larger institution, what feasibly can be developed by social work programs themselves?

3. What are the characteristics of faculty who choose to teach in DE programs? What characteristics, including special training in DE delivery, contribute to their success? To what extent are incentives important in their recruitment and retention?
4. How do the well-documented differences between DE and on-campus students, such as age and years of experience, affect the likelihood of success? Although we cannot change background characteristics, they could easily be used as control variables in the types of comparability analyses emphasized to date. This is especially feasible for those DE programs using the same instruments across several cohorts. Merge your datasets and you will have a large enough sample for regression analyses!
5. What funding sources are available and utilized? If DE courses cost more than on-campus courses, how much can the market bear?
6. How do CSWE accreditation standards contribute to or hinder the evolution of DE programs?

Throughput

Throughput involves a variety of factors related to program implementation, including recruitment and admissions processes, orientation processes for both students and faculty, learner-content interaction, learner-instructor interaction, learner-learner interaction, and learner-technology interaction. Student satisfaction with the quality of instruction and the availability and accessibility of support services could also be viewed as throughput factors as they affect actual learning outcomes. Faculty satisfaction could be viewed similarly. The following are questions for further research involving throughput factors.

1. What types of recruitment activities are successful? We know that a full room at a recruitment meeting does not necessarily translate into a large number of actual admissions applications. How do potential students hear about DE programs? How do we maintain their interest? How important are advertising, networking, involvement of DE alumni, and so on? What are their concerns about enrolling in a DE program (Hagan & Potts, 2000)?
2. Although DE programs must use admissions processes equivalent to those of the on-campus, per CSWE requirements, are

there particular criteria in need of attention for DE students, such as indispensable computer skills? What actually predicts success in DE (and other) programs such as GPAs, GREs, faculty ratings of personal statements, years of experience, and so on?

3. What do DE students need to know during orientation programs? What is the range of information presented currently? What modes of delivery are DE programs using to teach students basic survival skills, such as how to access electronic library databases?

4. What do DE faculty need to know before embarking on teaching at a distance? What training programs exist currently? How do faculty manage the extra preparation time needed (or perceived as needed)?

5. In terms of learner-content interaction, what types of pedagogy are used? What types are likely to be successful? How are they modified to meet the needs of distance learners? As noted by Macy et al. (2001), "we need to also ask what characteristics of teaching style are associated with success across formats (if any)" (p. 77). Is DE equally effective for teaching different content areas, such as human behavior, policy, research, and practice? What teaching styles are effective across different types of technologies?

6. In terms of learner-instructor interaction, how much is enough? How many site visits are sufficient for various types of courses? How much off-camera contact is required? How do faculties manage office hours? How does faculty cope with 24/7 e-mail accessibility?

7. In terms of learner-learner interaction, what is the extent of within-site peer support? How can the positive aspects of within-site support be maximized and any negative aspects be minimized? How can we minimize between-site conflict and promote healthy interactions?

8. In terms of learner-technology interaction, current knowledge is in its infancy, despite the proliferation of comparability evaluations. As stated earlier, an incredible variety of programs fall under the DE category: synchronous or nonsynchronous audio and/or video, with varying degrees of Web-based enhancement and varying degrees of in-person instruction. Updated descriptive studies of the modes of delivery used throughout the country would be valuable (Siegel & Jennings, 1998). A content

analysis of the existing comparability literature is also recommended.

Output

Output includes all types of proximal outcomes, such as academic performance, changes in values and attitudes, and skill development. These are the variables most commonly included in the existing DE evaluation literature. Much less is known about more distal outcomes, such as career trajectories among alumni. Studies of output variables tend also to focus on student-level outcomes, while much less is known about the impact of DE programs on faculty, host institutions, local agencies, local professional communities, and clients themselves. These gaps in our knowledge suggest obvious questions for further research.

1. Additional research should focus on the effects of various DE formats for specific types of courses. What are the strengths and weaknesses of various modes of delivery in terms of learning outcomes? Which types of courses are best suited for DE formats and for which types of formats? Beyond academic performance outcomes, what impacts do DE programs have on attitudes and values? What impacts do DE programs have on skill development?

2. More distal outcomes should be assessed, implying longer-term follow-up of DE alumni. To what extent are educational outcomes maintained over time? Has the DE experience changed practitioners' careers? To what extent do they engage in "professional socialization" activities?

3. DE may also impact faculty. What are faculty perceptions of personal and professional benefits? The assumption that good teachers do well in DE classrooms, while less gifted teachers do not, implies that teaching skills are not based on the mode of delivery. However, most DE faculty would agree that one "tries harder" because of the need to project over a distance (we cannot always rely on facial expressions and body language as feedback) and the desire to "look good" (we may be blessed or cursed by the opportunity to review our videotaped lectures). Preparation time may be increased due to the need to create supplementary materials. We may be more organized than usual due to the need to maximize valuable airtime. Are any of

these foreseeable improvements transferred to the traditional classroom? Similarly, what reward structures are appropriate for DE faculty? Are the standard course evaluations used by most universities appropriate for DE courses? Should nontenured professors risk teaching in such innovative programs? Seay, Rudolph, and Chamberlain (2001) discussed the effects on faculty of teaching in a non-social-work ITV program, including the impact of preparation time, incentives, and logistics. It was found that while faculty expected their teaching evaluations to be lower for DE courses, this was not the case in reality. Anecdotal concerns about lower student evaluations in DE courses should be recognized and addressed, particularly for those whose tenure depends in part on good evaluations.

4. Systems larger than the DE classroom should be examined, including the host institution. To what extent do DE programs benefit the host institution in terms of visibility, prestige, and funding? Or do DE programs drain resources from the host institution, for example, when the best and brightest faculty is drawn into DE teaching or when faculty resources are stretched thin to cover the addition of DE classes to the on-campus program?

5. Current research has only begun to consider the impact of DE programs on local communities. Do communities with DE programs experience an increase in the number of trained social workers? That is, do DE alumni remain in their communities and work in the field of human services? To what extent do local agencies benefit by the presence of interns and graduates?

6. Finally, to what extent do DE programs improve client well being? No comparability analyses have been conducted on client satisfaction or goal attainment, either of which would be feasible to assess. In a more perfect world, social work education as a whole would be able to answer this question.

CONCLUSION

Reflecting on the current emphasis on comparability analyses in the DE literature, Huff (2000) stated,

> Perhaps it is time for the comparisons to stop. Rather than continuing efforts to prove that distance education is as good as traditional

education, future research should simply focus on how to improve distance education courses by making them even more effective learning experiences for students. (p. 413)

Similarly, Coe and Gandy (1998) noted that such research should move beyond a deficits model (i.e., merely comparing DE programs against on-campus programs) to a strengths model (i.e., focusing on the particular strengths a DE program might offer).

As DE programs continue to evolve, and particularly as social work education moves toward Web-enhanced courses, Web-based courses, and entire Web-based degree programs, the challenge of creating a coherent body of knowledge will grow as well. What is now a literature based on apples, oranges, and plums may become a literature based on apples, oranges, plums, and grapes. However, with challenge comes opportunity. DE researchers are taking steps to collaborate across institutions, thus providing the opportunity to compare different modes of delivery within DE (e.g., Hollister & Kim, 2003; Potts & Kleinpeter, 2001). We are sharing instruments, thus providing the opportunity to amass larger datasets and to control for important input and throughput factors. We are beginning to attend to impacts on larger systems.

"It would behoove us to in social work education to think 'big picture' and to ask the same questions of our on-campus education efforts as we are doing with our distance programs" (Macy et al., 2001, p. 78). Although none of the "hard" (and few of the "easy") questions have been answered—such as the extent to which DE programs enhance professional socialization, help clients, or improve communities—it is expected that DE innovators will continue to lead the way toward understanding the processes and outcomes of social work education as a whole.

REFERENCES

Anderson. R., & Carter, I. (1990). *Human behavior in the social environment: A social systems approach* (4th ed.). New York: Aldine de Gruyter.

Bertalanffy, L. von. (1968). *General systems theory* (Rev. ed.). New York: Braziller.

Coe, J. R., & Elliot, D. (1999). An evaluation of teaching direct practice courses in a distance education program for rural settings. *Journal of Social Work Education, 35*, 353–365.

Coe, J. R., & Gandy, J. T. (1998, August). *Perspectives from consumers (students) in a distance education program.* Paper presented at the Conference on Information Technologies for Social Work Education and Practice, Charleston, SC.

Council on Social Work Education. (1994). *Accreditation standards.* [Online]. Available: http://CSWE.org. Retrieved August 1, 2003.

Council on Social Work Education. (2001). *Educational policy and accreditation Standards,* Final Version, November, 2002. [Online]. Available: http://CSWE.org. Retrieved August 1, 2003.

Council on Social Work Education. (2003). *Handbook of accreditation standards and procedures* (5th ed.). [Online]. Available: http://CSWE.org. Retrieved August 1, 2003.

Dalton, B. (2001). Distance education: A multidimensional evaluation. *Journal of Technology in Human Services, 18*(3-4), 101–115.

Forster, M., & Rehner, T. (1998). Part-time MSW distance education program: A program evaluation. *Computers in Human Services, 15*(2-3), 9–21.

Freddolino, P. P., & Sutherland, C. A. (2000). Assessing the comparability of classroom environments in graduate social work education delivered via interactive instructional television. *Journal of Social Work Education, 36,* 115–129.

Haagenstad, S., & Kraft, S. (1998, August). *Outcome measures comparing classroom education to distance education.* Paper presented at the Conference on Information Technologies for Social Work Education and Practice, Charleston, SC.

Haga, M., & Heitkamp, T. (2000). Bringing social work education to the prairie. *Journal of Social Work Education, 36,* 309–324.

Hagan, C. B., & Potts, M. K. (1999). The role of the site coordinator in a social work distance education program. *Professional Development: The International Journal of Continuing Social Work Education, 2*(3), 11–18.

Hagan, C. B., & Potts, M. K. (2000, August). Perceptions of entering MSW distance learners. Paper presented at the Conference on Information Technologies for Social Work Education and Practice, Charleston, SC.

Heitkamp, T. L. (1995, March). *Social work education at a distance: An innovative approach.* Paper presented at the Annual Program Meeting of the Council on Social Work Education, San Diego, CA.

Hillman, D. C., Willis, D. J., & Gunawardena, C. N. (1994). Learner interface interaction in distance education: An extension of contemporary models and strategies for practitioners. *The American Journal of Distance Education, 8*(2), 30–42.

Hollister, C. D., & Kim, Y. (2001). Evaluating ITV-based MSW programs: A comparison of ITV and traditional graduates' perceptions of MSW program qualities. *Journal of Technology in Human Services, 18*(1-2), 89–100.

Hollister, C. D., & Kim, Y. (2003, February-March). *Distance and traditional graduates' evaluation of MSW program support and educational outcomes.*

Paper presented at the Annual Program Meeting of the Council on Social Work Education, Atlanta, GA.

Hollister, C. D., & McGee, G. (1998, August). *Delivering substance abuse and child welfare content through interactive television.* Paper presented at the Conference on Information Technologies for Social Work Education and Practice. Charleston, SC.

Huff, M. T. (2000). A comparison study of live instruction versus interactive television for teaching MSW students critical thinking skills. *Research on Social Work Practice, 10,* 400–416.

Jennings, J., Siegel, E., & Conklin, J. J. (1995). Social work education and distance learning: Applications for continuing education. *Journal of Continuing Social Work Education, 6,* 3–7.

Kelley, P. (1993). Teaching through telecommunications. *Journal of Teaching in Social Work, 7,* 63–74.

Kikuchi, S. L., & Sorensen, S. R. (1997, September). *Reach out and touch someone: experiences of the rural off-campus MSW program, Graduate School of Social Work, University of Utah.* Paper presented at the Conference on Information Technologies for Social Work Education: Using to Teach, Teaching to Learn, Charleston, SC.

Kleinpeter, C. H., & Potts, M. K. (2000). Distance education: Teaching practice methods using interactive television. *Professional Development: The International Journal of Continuing Social Work Education, 3*(3), 37–43.

Kreuger, L. W., & Stretch, J. J. (1997, September). *Hyper-technology is destroying social work.* Paper presented at the Conference on Information Technologies for Social Work Education: Using to Teach, Teaching to Learn, Charleston, SC.

Kreuger, L. W., & Stretch, J. J. (2000). How hypermodern technology in social education bites back. *Journal of Social Work Education, 36,* 103–114.

Litzelfelner, P., Wiehe, V. R., & Olson, C. (2001). Distance education: The experiences of students and instructors in delivering a social work practice course via interactive TV. *Journal of Teaching in Social Work, 21,* 59–76.

Ligon, J., Markward, M. J., & Yegidis, B. L. (1997). Comparing student evaluation of distance learning and standard classroom courses in graduate social work education. Paper presented at the Annual Program Meeting of the Council on Social Work Education, Chicago, IL.

Macy, J. A. (1999, September). *Making the difference: Reports from distance MSW graduates regarding essential supports.* Paper presented at the Conference on Information Technologies for Social Work Education and Practice, Charleston, SC.

Macy, J. A., Rooney, R. H., Hollister, C. D., & Freddolino, P. P. (2001). Evaluation of distance education programs in social work. *Journal of Technology in Human Services, 18*(3-4), 63–84.

McFall, J. P., & Freddolino, P. P. (1998, August). *An overlooked outcome: The impact of distance education programs on community agencies.* Paper presented at the Conference on Information Technologies for Social Work Education and Practice, Charleston, SC.

McFall, J. P., & Freddolino, P. P. (2000a). The impact of distance education programs on community agencies. *Research on Social Work Practice, 10,* 438–454.

McFall, J. P., & Freddolino, P. P. (2000b). Quality and comparability in distance field education: Lessons learning from comparing three program sites. *Journal of Social Work Education, 36,* 293–307.

Mehrotra, C., Hollister, C. D., & McGahey, L. (2001). *Distance learning: Principles for design, delivery, and evaluation.* Thousand Oaks, CA: Sage.

Moore, M. G. (1989). Three types of interaction. *The American Journal of Distance Education, 3*(2), 1V6.

Moore, M. G., & Kearsley, G. (1996). *Distance education: A systems view.* Belmont, CA: Wadsworth.

Patchner, M. A., Petracchi, H., & Wise, S. (1997, September). Outcomes of ITV and face-to-faceinstruction in a social work research methods course. Paper presented at the Conference on Information Technologies for Social Work Education: Using to Teach, Teaching to Learn, Charleston, SC.

Petracchi, H. E., & Morgenbesser, M. (1994, March). *The use of video and one-way broadcast technology to deliver continuing social work education: A comparative assessment of student learning.* Paper presented at the Annual Program Meeting of the Council on Social Work Education, Atlanta, GA.

Petracchi, H. E., & Patchner, M. E. (2001a). A comparison of live instruction and interactive televised teaching: A 2-year assessment of teaching an MSW research methods course. *Research on Social Work Practice, 11,* 108–117.

Petracchi, H. E., & Patchner, M. E. (2001b). Student performance in three classroom settings: An evaluation of distance education. *Journal of Teaching in Social Work, 21,* 27–36.

Potts, M. K, & Hagan, C. B. (2000). Going the distance: Using systems theory to design, implement, and evaluate a distance education program. *Journal of Social Work Education, 36,* 131–145.

Potts, M. K., & Kleinpeter, C. B. (2003, February-March). *An evaluation of a five campus collaborative MSW program.* Paper presented at the Annual Program Meeting of the Council on Social Work Education, Atlanta, GA.

Potts, M. K., & Kleinpeter, C. H. (2001). Distance education alumni: How far have they gone? *Journal of Technology in Human Services, 18*(3–4), 85–99.

Raymond, F. B. (1988). Providing social work education and training in rural areas through interactive television. (ERIC Document Reproduction Services, No. 309910).

Rooney, R. H., Izaksonas, E., & Macy, J. A. (1998). Reframing from site bias to site identity: Pedagogic issues in delivering social work courses via interactive television. *Journal of Technology in Human Services, 16*(2-3), 175–192.

Seay, R., Rudolph, M. R., & Chamberlain, D. H. (2001). Faculty perceptions of interactive television instruction. *Journal of Education for Business, 77*(2), 99–105.

Sheafor, B. W. (1994). *Distance social work education for rural America: One small step in addressing rural poverty.* Paper presented at the Annual Program Meeting of the Council on Social Work Education, Atlanta, GA.

Siegel, E., & Jennings, J. G. (1998). Distance learning in social work education: Results and implications of a national study. *Journal of Social Work Education, 34,* 71–80.

Thyer, B. A., Artelt, T., Markward, M. K., & Dozier, C. D. (1998). Evaluating distance learning in social work education: A replication study. *Journal of Social Work Education, 34,* 291–295.

Verduin, J. R., & Clark, T. A. (1991). *Distance education: The foundations of effective practice.* San Francisco: Jossey-Bass.

Chapter 8

FACULTY ISSUES IN DISTANCE EDUCATION

Jo Ann R. Coe Regan, Ph.D.

Distance education is the term used to describe those formal teacher-learner arrangements in which the teacher and learner are geographically separated most or all of the time and the communication between them is through a technology medium such as audiocassette, telephone, radio, television, computers, interactive videodisc and print (Blakely, 1994; Conklin & Ostendorf; 1995; Kahl & Cropley, 1986; Verduin & Clark, 1991). Distance education is not a new concept but is considered an innovative approach to delivering education services due to the recent technological advances in the areas of computers, multimedia, and television (Walsh, 1993). In the last 5 years, the increased use of the computer, Internet, and course management software systems has resulted in the development of technology-supported learning environments and particularly online distance-education programs. These advances have provided educators with a wide variety of electronic tools to assist them in creating many more opportunities for institutions of higher education to offer distance education programs.

As institutions of higher education have developed distance education programs, faculty in these programs has responded with a range of attitudes and perceptions regarding these innovative instructional tools. The importance of users' and potential users' attitudes in the implementation of any new innovation such as distance education has been documented as being important to the success or failure of an innovation (Mort, 1951; Rogers & Jain, 1968). The support and involvement of the faculty as well as their attitudes, whether positive or negative, has been documented as being critical to the effectiveness of any distance learning program (Beaudoin, 1990; Dillon, 1989). As McNeil (1990) states, "the attitudinal issues—how people perceive and react to these technologies—are far more important now than the structural and technical obstacles in influencing the use of technology in higher education" (p. 2). Schrock (1985) found that negative faculty attitudes resulted in intentional and unintentional sabotage of distance education programs. Lewis and Wall (1990) found that when faculty felt fearful or intimidated by distance learning, they were reluctant to use such systems or provided ineffective instruction. A 1999 national survey of information technology in U.S. higher education found the single most important information technology (IT) challenge in higher education is assisting faculty on how to integrate technology into instruction (Green, 1999).

Given the important role faculty have in planning, implementing, and delivering distance education programs, this chapter will focus on (a) a review of the literature regarding faculty involvement in distance education; (b) identifying important issues facing faculty involved in distance education programs; and (c) making recommendations for dealing with these issues.

REVIEW OF LITERATURE ON FACULTY ISSUES IN DISTANCE EDUCATION

There have been few studies on faculty and distance education despite the fact that the literature in distance education emphasizes the support and involvement of the faculty as necessary to designing a distance education program (Beaudoin, 1990). This is unfortunate as faculty are in the best position to accept or reject educational innovations proposed by administration or governing boards (Cowen & Brawer, 1989; Walker, 1976). Generally, the research concerning faculty issues is divided into two broad areas: barriers and motives regarding faculty involvement in distance education, and faculty attitudes and perceptions toward distance education (Walsh, 1993).

Dillon and Walsh (1992) reviewed 225 articles dealing with distance education and found only 24 research studies focused on faculty issues. The majority of this research was concerned with barriers and motives, including the level of institutional faculty support and training opportunities for faculty (Beaudoin, 1990; Blackburn & Ging, 1986; Clark, Soliman, & Sangaila, 1985; Cyrs, 1989; Cyrs & Smith, 1990; Dillon, 1989; Dillon, Hengst, & Zoller, 1991; Farr, Murphy, & Flatt, 1992; Flinn, 1991; Gilcher & Johnstone, 1989; Grossman, 1989; Johnson & Silvernail, 1990; Kirby & Garrison, 1989; Kromholz & Johnstone, 1988; LeBlanc, 1992; Mani, 1988; Okimoto & Metcalf, 1991; Parer, 1988; Purdy & Icenogle, 1976; Seay, Rudolph, & Chamberlain, 2001; Scriven, 1986; Siaciwena, 1989; Smith, 1991; Taylor & White, 1991). Generally these studies concluded the following regarding support, barriers and motives regarding distance education:

- Faculty who teach distance education courses felt positive about the experience (Beaudoin, 1990; Dillon, 1989; Johnson & Silvernail, 1990; Mani, 1988; Parer, 1988; Purdy & Icenogle, 1976; Taylor & White, 1991).
- As faculty increase their involvement with distance education teaching and technology, attitudes about the experience became more positive (Gilcher & Johnstone, 1989; Kirby & Garrison, 1989; Seay et al., 2001).
- Training of faculty on the use of distance education has involved use of graphics, promoting interaction, managing the equipment, on-camera presentation, use of questioning techniques, and learning assessment (Clark et al., 1985; Cyrs & Smith, 1990; Dillon et al., 1991; Scriven, 1986; Siaciwena, 1989).
- Common supports provided to distance education instructors have been increased compensation, teaching assistants, instructional and course materials design, technical support, and training opportunities for faculty (Cyrs, 1989; Dillon, 1989; Flinn, 1991; Kromholz & Johnstone, 1988; Okimoto & Metcalf, 1991; Parer, 1988; Smith, 1991).
- Factors contributing to being most helpful to faculty include assistance in preparing course materials, clerical support, assistance in communicating with distance education students; marketing and distribution of course materials, and institutional support (Blackburn & Ging, 1986; Dillon, 1989; Grossman, 1989; LeBlanc, 1992; Okimoto & Metcalf, 1991).
- Barriers to teaching distance education courses have included lack of time and inadequate rewards for distance efforts as well

as the concern that poor teaching methods may be highlighted in distance education mode (Farr et al., 1992).

- Distance learning requires increased responsibilities such as (a) utilization of different teaching strategies to overcome the lack of face-to-face interaction and (b) adopting course materials for teaching at a distance (Cafarella, Dunning, & Patrick, 1992; Cyrs & Smith, 1990).

The other groups of studies have addressed faculty attitudes and perceptions toward a particular distance education technology or process recently used as well as faculty members' attitudes and perceptions towards distance education issues in general (Annenberg CPB Project, 1986; Burnham, 1988; Chute & Balthazar, 1988; Clark et al., 1985; Dillon, 1988; Dillon et al., 1991; Holloway, 1975; Johnson & Silvernail, 1990; McNeil, 1990; Parer, 1988; Purdy & Icengole, 1976; Schrock, 1985; Scriven, 1986; Siaciwena, 1989; Taylor & White, 1991). Surveys have been the primary data collection tool and conclusions drawn by researchers in these studies include the following:

- Negative faculty attitudes toward distance education have focused on workload questions, time involved, student spontaneity and interaction, and technical and administrative problems (Clark et al., 1985; Dillon et al., 1991; Johnson & Silvernail, 1990; McNeil, 1990; Parer, 1988; Scriven, 1986; Siaciwena, 1989).
- Senior-level faculty, rather than those in lesser ranks, tend to have more positive attitudes about distance education teaching in terms of being more enjoyable and challenging (Clark et al., 1985; Dillon, 1988a; Purdy & Icenogle, 1976).
- Most of the empirical research on faculty attitudes towards distance education has been limited to faculty who have had exposure to distance education programs. Generally, the more exposure faculty have had, the more likely they will have positive attitude towards the use of distance education. However, these studies have not compared those who have not had experience with distance education (Annenberg CPB Project, 1986; Burnham, 1988; Chute & Balthazar, 1988; Holloway, 1975; Schrock, 1985; Taylor & White, 1991).

The most comprehensive study on faculty attitudes toward distance education is by Clark (1987) who conducted a national survey of faculty at public U.S. institutions of higher education on their attitudes toward college-credit distance education. At that time, Clark found that faculty had slightly positive attitudes toward distance education as a general concept, slightly to moderately positive attitudes toward the development and distribution of distance education by their institution, and negative attitudes toward implementing distance education in their own program and personally using this as a medium of instruction. Clark also found that 2-year college and comprehensive university faculty held more positive attitudes about distance education than research university faculty. To date, this has been the only national study but only three disciplines were represented in the study: chemistry, marketing, and political science.

For the most part, empirical data on the attitudes and perceptions of faculty toward distance education are scarce and have been primarily post-hoc assessments of faculty who have taught distance education courses (Walsh, 1993). The majority of these studies are descriptive rather than empirical. They have small sample sizes as they primarily concentrate on faculty who have utilized distance education. However, they do provide descriptive information regarding faculty involved in distance education.

SUMMARY OF FACULTY PERCEPTIONS IN SOCIAL WORK EDUCATION

Several studies in the social work literature address faculty perceptions (Forster & Washington, 2000; Freddolino, 1996(a), 1996(b); Haga & Heitkamp, 2000; Raymond, 1996; Weinbach, Gandy, & Tartaglia, 1984). Most of these studies were evaluation studies of distance education projects that include surveys of participating faculty regarding such issues as support, faculty attitudes, and barriers and motives to utilizing distance education

The studies reviewed indicate that social work faculty generally supported the use of distance learning. Though most of them express initial trepidation, they accepted it more as they gained experience utilizing distance education. Weinbach (1985) surveyed faculty with a pre- and-post-test attitudinal survey before they taught on television and afterwards. Although 75% expressed concerns about this method of teaching, afterwards 100% supported this as an effective teaching medium. Other studies (Freddolino, 1996(a), 1996(b); Haga & Heitkamp, 2000) have also found that 100% of the faculty who have taught in the distance learning program supported the use of this type of learning in social work education and reported a high level of satisfaction with teaching distance education courses. Although these studies are small in number, these findings are consistent with other studies in the distance education literature indicating that as faculty increase their involvement with distance education teaching and technology, attitudes about the experience become more positive (Dillon, 1989; Gilcher & Johnstone, 1989; Johnson & Silvernail, 1990; Kirby & Garrison, 1989; Mani, 1988; Parer, 1988; Taylor & White, 1991). Three studies reviewed in the social work literature indicated negative faculty attitudes toward distance education (Freddolino, 1996a; Haga & Heitkamp, 2000; Rompf, 1999). All the studies identified concerns from faculty on technology problems such as quality of the video and audio signal, capacity of the compressed video system, and loss of time to technology. Other concerns from faculty included loss of personal contact with students and the teaching of practice classes via distance. Faculty found it more difficult to assign grades to students they did not know as well as students they saw in class each week. Other studies reviewed in other academic disciplines have indicated negative attitudes (Clark et al., 1985; Dillon et al., 1991; Johnson & Silvernail, 1990; McNeil, 1990; Parer, 1988; Scriven, 1986; Siaciwena, 1989) around similar issues particularly in the area of technical and administrative problems. Other negative issues have focused on workload questions, time involved, and student spontaneity and interaction. Haga & Heitkamp (2000) reported more difficulty in maintaining relationships with distance education students than with traditional students.

Another study has also looked at faculty preparation issues. Raymond (1996) reported that most faculty teaching in distance education "overprepared" when teaching on television and had to make greater use of audio-visual materials. Haga & Hietkamp (2000) found in their evaluations of distance education programs that faculty had to be more organized and prepared when teaching at a distance. Other studies indicate that distance teaching requires additional skills to be effective beyond those in the traditional face-to-face classroom situation. For example, the use of graphics, promoting interaction, managing the equipment, the use of questioning techniques, and learning assessment as well as on-camera presentation have been rated differently by faculty teaching in distance learning programs (Cyrs & Smith, 1990; Gilcher & Johnstone, 1989). Studies in other disciplines have indicated that senior-level faculty, rather than those in lesser ranks, tend to teach in distance learning programs because they found it more challenging (Verduin & Clark, 1991). Other literature on programmatic concerns (Blakely, 1994; Blakely & Schoenherr, 1995) has discussed opinions of faculty in schools of social work on what types of courses should be offered via distance education. Although the empirical studies reviewed do include practice courses, none of the studies discussed which courses faculty thought more appropriate for teaching via interactive television. However, there is some concern in the social work literature about practice courses as it has not been definitively demonstrated whether teaching practice courses is appropriate (Blakely, 1994; Rompf, 1999).

An examination of study methodologies on faculty perceptions indicate that the scientific rigor of the studies needs to be improved in order to assess faculty perceptions on the use of distance learning in social work education. All of studies reviewed have small sample sizes of faculty who only have taught in distance education programs which makes it difficult to generalize findings. Only one study (Weinbach, 1985) indicates a pre- and post-test of faculty attitudes prior to distance teaching. The other studies have been post-hoc assessments of whether faculty support this as an effective teaching medium.

The studies reviewed appear to concentrate on whether faculty support the use of distance teaching. Although the three studies reviewed indicate positive support on the use of distance teaching in social work education, it seems that there should be more systematic research on social work faculty perceptions. For example, there are no studies that compare the attitudes of those faculty who teach in distance learning programs with those who do not. Also, there are no studies on the type of social work educators are most appropriate for producing quality distance education programs. Most of the findings concentrate on positive faculty attitudes but further research is needed on negative attitudes to assess how this can influence the use of distance teaching. Also, none of the studies were national in scope or representative of social work faculty as a whole.

DIFFUSION OF INNOVATION THEORY

In order to understand how distance education as an innovative educational delivery mode has diffused, a theoretical and conceptual framework by Rogers (1983) is often used to describe faculty and their role in distance education. Much has been written on how and why different innovations may or may not be adopted. Gabriel Tarde

(1903) wrote, "Our problem is to learn why, given one hundred different innovations conceived of at the same time—innovations in the form of words, in mythological idea, in industrial processes, etc.—ten will spread abroad while ninety will be forgotten" (p. 140). The results of technological change are everywhere in household products, automation, medicine, and every type of industry. Despite the number of technological changes, there exists a considerable time lag before a technological innovation is accepted. For example, hybrid corn seed was not adopted completely in Iowa until 14 years after its invention. New educational practices are said to take 25 years before they are implemented in the average American school (Rogers, 1983). For this reason, diffusion research has been used to determine methods on how diffusion can be hastened as well as serve as a predictive tool for how an innovation can be implemented. Diffusion research has been used in a variety of settings to understand the diffusion of a myriad of ideas. For example, more than 172 different research studies dealing with educational innovations have been completed since 1938 (Rogers, 1983). Rural sociologists have completed diffusion studies on how agricultural techniques are adopted by farmers. Rogers (1983) found 506 diffusion studies on a variety of innovations such as medicine, driver's training, and technical products that investigated how these innovations were adopted. Although every behavioral science has some interest in the diffusion of new ideas, six major diffusion traditions are examined by Rogers (1983). They include anthropology, early sociology, rural sociology, education, industrial, and medical sociology. The education diffusion tradition is one of the largest in terms of studies, as many scholars have investigated what causes new educational innovations to be adopted in practice. Diffusion theory is applicable to understanding how faculty perceives distance education as an innovative educational tool.

Rogers (1983), the leading diffusion researcher, introduces several concepts important to understanding diffusion of innovation theory. An innovation is "an idea, practice, or product that is perceived as new by an individual or other unit of adoption" (p. 13). Diffusion is "the process by which an innovation spreads," and diffusion process is "the spread of a new idea from its source of invention or creation to its ultimate users or adopters" (p. 13). An adopter is "an individual who has employed or used an innovation" and usually exists in a social system that "comprises a population of individuals who are functionally differentiated and engaged in problem-solving behavior." Adoption is a "decision to continue full use of an innovation," while the adoption process is "the mental process through which an individual passes from first hearing about an innovation to final adoption." Innovativeness is "the degree to which an individual is relatively earlier in adopting new ideas from other members of his/her social system" (p. 20).

The research in diffusions of innovations has primarily focused on communication in the diffusion process and can be divided into three areas: (a) communication networks (Rogers, 1973; Rogers & Jain, 1968; Rogers & Kincaid, 1981); (b) the relative influence of individuals within an organization (Rogers, 1983; Rogers & Kincaid, 1981; Rogers & Shoemaker, 1971); and (c) the comparative influence of interpersonal and mass media communication (Rogers, 1983; Rogers, Rogers, Daley, & Wu, 1982; Rogers, & Lee, 1975). In all three of these areas, the importance of the message is emphasized in the communication process (Walsh, 1993). Rogers (1962, 1983) and Rogers and Shoemaker (1971) divide this message into five objective elements that are characteristics of the innovation:

1. Relative advantage is "the degree to which an innovation is perceived as better than the idea or method it supersedes."
2. Compatibility is "the degree to which an innovation is consistent with existing values, past experiences and needs of the adopters."
3. Complexity is "the degree to which an innovation is relatively difficult to understand and use."
4. Trialability is "the degree to which an innovation may be experimented with on a limited basis."
5. Observability is "the degree to which the results of an innovation are visible to others."

Rogers (1983) cites several innovation studies that lend support to the applicability of these innovation attributes (Clinton, 1973; Elliott, 1968; Hahn, 1974; Holloway, 1975; Kivlin, 1960). These studies found that the characteristics of relative advantage, compatibility, and complexity received strong support in these studies while trialability and observability were less supported. However, a number of studies in the educational literature have tested the applicability of the five characteristcs to different educational innovations. Levine (1978, 1980) found support for the characteristics of compatibility and relative advantage in his studies on why an experimental college was implemented in one major university but not at another. Brew (1982) studied the individual perceptions of faculty towards the adoption of open-university course materials at a conventional British university. She found that all of the innovational attributes in faculty explained whether or not faculty had a positive or negative attitude regarding the adoption of these course materials.

OTHER DIFFUSION STUDIES

Buckles (1989), Pittman (1994), and Coe (2000) looked at what variables were associated with the diffusion of information technology among social work faculty. Utilizing Rogers' (1983) theory of diffusion of innovations, each looked at the characteristics of institutions, individuals, and innovations in determining what impacts the diffusion of computer innovation amongst social work faculty. Buckles found that innovational attributes explained the diffusion of information technology amongst social work faculty more significantly than individual or institutional attributes. Pittman also looked at innovational attributes amongst social work faculty in determining whether or not social work faculty adopted computers as instructional tools. She also utilized Rogers' (1983) theory of diffusion of innovations to identify which attributes of innovation would most likely be correlated with adoption of computers as instructional tools while controlling for institutional and individual attributes. Her study found that the perceptions of innovational attributes were moderate predictors of instructional innovations in determining what impacts the diffusion of computer innovation amongst social work faculty. Coe surveyed 428 social work faculty in the United States on why or why not faculty would adopt the use of television and the Internet as an instructional tool. She found that innovational and institutional attributes were significantly associated with the adoption of television and the Internet as instructional tools while individual attributes were not. Organizational support was the most significant predictor of adoption by social work faculty.

RELEVANT ISSUES FOR FACULTY INVOLVED IN DISTANCE EDUCATION

Most studies reviewed indicate that perceptions by faculty are related to usage and likelihood of usage of distance education media as instructional tools. This is important to the design and implementation of distance education programs. It is important that before implementing any distance education media in teaching, faculty need to perceive the innovational attributes of these media positively. For example, it is important that faculty perceive a relative advantage dimension of these media. This dimension can include such things as rewards, benefits, and the need for using distance education media in their teaching. It must also be compatible with their values and belief systems about education and teaching philosophies. Other literature review findings also suggest that it is important that faculty have opportunities to experiment and observe the results of using distance education media in their teaching. Most findings indicate that as faculty increase their experience with distance education media, they were more likely to indicate they had used or were willing to use these media in their teaching. It is also important that faculty do not perceive these media as too complex to use or understand. The media utilized in a distance education program must be easy to use and clear in meaning in order for faculty to use or be willing to use in their teaching.

Other findings indicated that institutional support is important to usage and willingness to use distance education media. Studies indicate that institutions with climates and processes supportive to the innovation were more likely to adopt the use of distance education media in their teaching (Ging, 1986; Hendrick, 1986). Other studies (Rogers, 1983; Rogers & Shoemaker, 1971) found that factors such as size, system openness, specialization, funds, and structure of an institution impacts the diffusion of innovations. However, both of these studies discuss that these variables tend to be more complex in that they require observation and surveying institutional leaders to assess how culture impacts this diffusion. The literature reviewed does suggest that if the institution is not supportive of distance education, then the faculty will not be using or willing to use distance education media in their teaching. Many studies reviewed indicated that faculty had an interest in utilizing distance education media but would not get any institutional support for this type of teaching. Also, there is very little in the current tenure system structure that rewards this type of innovation in teaching.

Other findings indicate that organizational support and planning are also associated with usage of distance education media. Studies have found that an organization must provide rewards, incentives, and technical support to members involved in the implementation of an innovation (Rothman, 1974; Seay et al., 2001). Other studies have also looked at the importance of involving organization members in the development of a plan for the innovation as well as communicating the plan for implementing the innovation with all members of the organization. These findings suggest that the more universities and colleges involve their faculty in the development and planning of distance education, the more likely faculty will be involved in distance education. It also means that it is important that departments communicate the plans for distance education and offer rewards, incentives, and supports to faculty for being involved in distance education.

RECOMMENDATIONS

The review of the literature regarding faculty and distance education leads to several recommendations as they relate to the design, implementation and planning for distance education courses:

Planning and Preparation Issues

It is important that programs planning to initiate or expand distance education courses focus on how faculty perceives the innovational attributes of the distance education media. Training and program planning that focuses on these innovational attributes will help to enhance perceptions of relative advantage, compatibility, complexity, trialability, and observability and encourage the use and likelihood of usage of the distance education media by faculty. In a national survey of distance learning in social work education, Siegel and Jennings (1998) found that some of the barriers to establishing a distance education program are philosophical. They found in their survey of faculty that distance learning was viewed with suspicion and as a nontraditional method of teaching that needs to be viewed with caution. Many faculty cited concerns about the perceived quality of classroom interaction, the potential socialization of students, and the relationship of the instructor as a mentor and role model. They also found that because of these philosophical views, many faculty may not be able to make a paradigm shift from the traditional classroom to one that uses distance education media. To encourage the use and likelihood of use of these media by all faculty in a higher education program, it is necessary to involve all faculty in training that focuses on the perceptions regarding the innovational attributes of the distance education media; and (b) provide the supports for faculty involved in these programs. Often, programs focus on recruiting certain individuals with an interest in teaching distance education. Training also needs to be instituted by the accrediting bodies such as the Council on Social Work Education (CSWE). CSWE has supported this area in recent years with a symposium at their development of a conference in this area and publish a special issue of research studies on distance education. All of these activities help to focus on changing perceptions about innovational attributes and can encourage usage and likelihood of usage of distance education media by all faculty. This is particularly relevant given the increased growth and push in recent years by institutions of higher learning to develop distance education programs.

Despite the philosophical barriers identified in the literature, none of these barriers seem related to any particular demographic characteristic of faculty. Programs planning to initiate and expand the use of distance education can involve all levels of rank, age, gender, ethnicity, educational background, and status of faculty to be involved in the implementation of distance education teaching. However, it is clear that training initiatives focused on developing familiarity with distance education media are essential to overcoming any of these barriers. Forster and Washington (2000) found that being comfortable with technology and flexibility in applying the technology are two of the most important areas for faculty development. They found that faculty who already use a variety of instructional strategies require the least faculty development and are least resistant to utilizing distance education media in their teaching. Faculty who rely on more traditional methods of teaching (i.e., lecture) will require more development and change in certain areas. They cite Gottschalk's (2003) checklist of behaviors that faculty must develop to enhance their effectiveness with distance education media. These include nonverbal behavior, use of humor, and control and pace of the classroom. Cyrs (1989) also includes skills such as teamwork, questioning strategies, and coordination of teaching activities when a faculty member has several distance education sites.

It is important that social work programs include faculty in their planning and development of distance education courses. They must also include rewards, incentives, and support for faculty involved in these programs. Administrators must also identify organizational supports to encourage the use of these media by faculty. For example, financial and workload incentives should be provided to individual faculty who choose to adopt this media in their teaching. These incentives could include overload pay, double-course unit credit, and course reductions. Other supports include technical support, financial support for the hardware and software needed to develop distance education courses. Seay and colleagues (2001) found that institutions wanting to develop distance education programs must make a financial commitment to ensure success. Financial commitments include up-to-date and functioning equipment as well as release time and training to convert courses to a format that utilizes distance education media. Faculty stipends are considered a good incentive for participation. Clear guidelines in the tenure and promotion structure also need to be considered for those faculty who are developing and implementing distance education courses in their teaching.

Traing and Technical Assistance

Faculty development is a key issue identified in many of the studies reviewed (Forster & Washington, 2000; Green, 1999; Potts & Hagan, 2000). All of the studies recommend the importance of a formal orientation and faculty development program for all faculty teaching in distance education programs. Forster and Washington found that it is important to include hands-on training with the actual technology and how-to guides for course redesign, use of graphics, and student engagement. They recommend a number of resources to assist with this orientation (Cyrs & Smith, 1990; Hanson et al., 1997; Ostendorf, 1994) as well as university Web sites such as the University of Wisconsin (www.uwex.edu/disted) and the University of Maryland (www. umuc.edu/ide). They also utilize mentoring support to "neophytes and technophobes" and early course observation and formative evaluations on faculty performance so that faculty can make adjustments in their teaching style.

Siegel and Jennings (1998) found in their survey that faculty have to use more visuals such as illustrations, graphics, and videotapes along with maintaining interaction with students at various sites. Technical assistance is identified as one of the crucial areas for support because most faculty do not have degrees in education and little experience with technology in their teaching. Given the increased skills in teaching, it is important that technical assistance be provided to faculty so they can focus on the added skills to teach in the distance learning classroom.

Organizational ane Institutional Support

Given the importance of organizational and institutional support found in the studies reviewed, it is important that higher education institutions focus on how to provide the supports needed for the adoption of distance education. Institutions need to focus on developing a vision for why distance education is needed. For example, the rationale for having distance education at one university is the vision by the state legislatures that everyone in their state should have access to higher education within 25 miles from their home. This type of vision fits well with social work programs' mission of empowering groups that traditionally do not have access to education such as women and persons in rural areas. It also focuses on the importance of the political process that can encourage the use of distance education at a systems level. Also, the organizational structure needs to be supportive of faculty who are utilizing distance education media in their teaching. Curriculum committees must provide guidance and supportive processes for faculty who are interested in teaching distance education courses. For example, one social work program appoints a faculty member on the curriculum committee to represent distance education and technology as one of the content areas.

CONCLUSION

The review of the literature indicates that there are a number of faculty in institutions and programs who are interested in utilizing the distance education media in their teaching. This indicates that distance education programs can continue to grow, with more faculty adopting the use of these media in their teaching. It is this group of educators who can take the lead and pave the way for new advances in higher education. Future challenges facing higher education can be addressed with advances in the use of distance education. The focus of this chapter was to identify and discuss important faculty issues to consider in the design, planning, and implementation of successful distance learning programs. The growth of online education will only continue to advance the use of distance education in higher education further. The challenge for the next century will be in designing the training and support mechanisms to help faculty in this endeavor.

REFERENCES

Annenberg CPB Project. (1986). *Faculty perspectives on the role of information technologies in academic instruction.* Washington, DC: Corporation for Public Broadcasting.

Beaudoin, M. (1990). The instructor's changing role in distance education. *American Journal of Distance Education, 4*(2), 21–29.

Blackburn, R. T., & Ging, T. (1986). *Faculty and administrator use of Annenberg/CPB project video courses.* Washington, DC: Educational Testing Service for the Annenberg/CPB Project.

Blakely, T. J. (1994). Strategies for distance learning. *Journal of Continuing Social Work Education, 6*(1), 4–6.

Blakely, T. J. & Schoenherr, P. (1995). Telecommunications technologies in social work distance education. *Journal of Continuing Social Work Education, 6*(3), 8–12.

Brew, A. (1982). The process of innovation in university teaching. *British Journal of Educational Technology, 13*(2), 153–162.

Buckles, B. J. (1989). *Identification of variables influencing the readiness to implement information technology by social work faculty.* Unpublished doctoral dissertation, Adelphi University, New York.

Burnham, B. R. (1988). *An examination of the perceptions and motivations of faculty participating in a distance education project.* Paper presented at the Fourth Annual Conference on Teaching at a Distance. Madison, WI: School of Education.

Cafarella, R. S., Dunning, B., & Patrick, S. (1992). Delivering off-campus instruction: Changing roles and responsibilities of professors in higher education. *Continuing Higher Education Review, 56*(3), 155–165.

Chute, A. G. & Balthazar, L. B. (1988). *An overview of research and development projects at the AT & T national teletraining center.* Cincinnati, OH: AT&T National Teletraining Center. (ERIC Document Reproductive Service No. ED313018)

Clark, T. A. (1987). *Faculty attitudes toward distance education in U.S. public higher education.* Unpublished doctoral dissertation, Southern Illinois University at Carbondale.

Clark, R., Soliman, M., & Sangaila, H. (1985). Staff perceptions of external versus internal teaching and staff development. *Distance Education, 5*(1), 84–92.

Clinton, A. (1973). *A study of the attributes of educational innovations as factors in diffusion.* Unpublished doctoral dissertation, University of Toronto, Canada.

Coe, J. R. (2000). *Factors predicting social work faculty participation in distance education media Television and the internet.* Unpublished doctoral dissertation, University of Texas at Arlington.

Conklin, J. J., Jennings, J., & Siegel, E. (1993). *The use of technology as an enhancement to teaching distance education.* Paper presented at a Faculty Development Institute, Council on Social Work Education Annual Program Meeting, Atlanta, GA.

Cowen, A. M., & Brawer, F. B. (1989). *The American community college.* San Francisco: Jossey-Bass.

Cyrs, T. E. (1989). Designing a teleclass instructor's workshop addressing the differential skills needed for quality teleclass teaching. *Proceedings of the Fifth Annual Conference on Teaching at a Distance* (pp. 178–183). Madison, WI: School of Education.

Cyrs, T. E. & Smith, M. (1990). *Teleclass teaching: A resource guide* (2nd ed.). Las Cruces: New Mexico State University.

Dillon, C. (1989). Faculty rewards and instructional telecommunications: A view from the telecourse facility. *American Journal of Distance Education, 3*(2), 35–43.

Dillon, C., Hengst, D., & Zoller, D. (1991). Instructional strategies and student involvement in distance education: A study of the Oklahoma Televised Instructional System. *Journal of Distance Education, 6*(1), 28–41.

Dillon, C., & Walsh, S. (1992). Faculty: The neglected resource in distance education. *American Journal of Distance Education, 6*(3), 5–21.

Elliott, J. G. (1968). *Farmers' perceptions of innovations as related to self-concept and adoption.* Unpublished doctoral dissertation, Michigan State University. East Lansing, MI.

Farr, C. W., Murphy, K. L., & Flatt, L.W. (1992). Overcoming inherent obstacles: How to convince recalcitrant faculty to do what's best. *Proceedings from the Eighth Annual Conference on Distance Teaching and Learning* (pp. 45–49). Madison, WI: School of Education.

Flinn, W. (1991). A team approach to designing, producing, and teaching distance education courses. *Proceedings from the Seventh Annual Conference on Distance Teaching and Learning* (pp. 36–39). Madison, WI: School of Education.

Forster, M., & Washington, E. (2000). A model for developing and managing distance education programs using interactive video technology. *Journal of Social Work Education, 36*(1), 147–159.

Freddolino, P. P (1996a). Maintaining quality in graduate social work programs delivered to distant sites using electronic instruction technology. In E. T. Reck (Ed.), *Modes of professional education II: The electronic social work curriculum in the twenty-first century. Tulane Studies in Social Welfare,* 20. New Orleans, LA: Tulane University.

Freddolino, P. P. (1996b). The importance of relationships for a quality learning environment in Interactive tv classroom. *Journal of Education for Business, 71*(4), 205–208.

Gilcher, K., & Johnstone, S. (1989). A critical review of the use of audiographic conferencing systems by selected educational institutions. *International Universities Consortium*, College Park: University of Maryland.

Ging, T. J. (1986). *Diffusion of instructional television in higher education: A study of the Annenberg/CPB Project.* Unpublished doctoral dissertation, University of Michigan. East Lansing, MI.

Gottschalk, T. H. (Ed.). (2003, May). *Instructional development for distance education. Distance Education at a glance guide #3.* University of Idaho College of Engineering. Web site:: http://www.uidaho.edu/eo/dist3.html.

Green, K. C. (1999). *The continuing challenge of instructional integration and user support.* Campus Computing. Web site:: http://www.campuscomputing.net.

Grossman, D. (1989). Distance education: Consolidating the gains. *Proceedings from the Fifth Annual Conference on Distance Teaching and Learning* (pp. 28–39). Madison, WI: School of Education.

Haga, M., & Heitkamp, T. L. (2000). Bringing social work education to the prairie. *Journal of Social Work Education, 36*(2), 309–324.

Hahn, C. L. (1974). *Relationships between potential adopters' perceptions of social studies innovations and their adoptions of these innovations in Indiana, Ohio, Georgia, and Florida.* Unpublished doctoral dissertation, Indiana University at Bloomington.

Hanson, D., Maushak, N. J., Schlosser, C. A., Anderson, M. L., Sorenson, C., Simonson, M. (1997). *Distance education: Review of the literature* (2nd ed.). Washington, DC: Association for Educational Communications.

Hendrick, L. C. (1986). *Knowledge about and attitude toward instructional television: A survey of the faculty and the administrators in the Los Rios Community College district.* Unpublished doctoral dissertation, University of San Francisco.

Holloway, R. E. (1975). *Perceived attributes of an innovation: Syracuse University project advance.* Paper presented at the Annual Meeting of the American Educational Research Association, Washington, DC.

Johnson, J., & Silvernail, D. (1990). *Report of faculty perceptions of Community College of Maine Instructional Television System,* Fall 1989, University of Southern Maine.

Kahl, T. N., & Cropley, A. J. (1986). Face to face versus distance learning: Psychological consequences and practical implications, *Distance Education, 7,* 38–48.

Kirby, D., & Garrison, D. (1989). Graduate distance education: A study of the aims and delivery systems. In *Proceedings from the Eighth Annual Conference of the Canadian Association for the Study of Adult Education* (pp. 179–84). Cornwall, Ontario: Saint Lawrence College of Saint Laurent.

Kivlin, J. E. (1960). *Characteristics of farm practices associated with rate of adoption.* Unpublished doctoral dissertation, Pennsylvania State University. University Park.

Kromholz, S. F., & Johnstone, S. M. (1988). A practical guide to training instructional television faculty and students. *Lifelong Learning: An Omnibus of Practice and Research, 11*(8), 15–18.

LeBlanc, G. (1992). Bridging the distance: Supporting distance education faculty and staff at the University of Maine. *Proceedings from the Eighth Annual Conference on Distance Teaching and Learning* (pp. 94–98). Madison, WI: School of Education.

Levine, A. (1978). *The life and death of innovation in higher education.* Buffalo, NY: Department of Higher Education Studies, State University of New York.

Levine, A. (1980). *Why innovation fails.* Albany, NY: State University of New York.

Lewis, R. L., & Wall, M. (1990). Wiring the ivory tower: A round table on technology in higher education. *Proceedings from the Conference of the Academy for Educational Development* (pp. 9–27). Washington, DC: Publications Department. (ERIC Document Reproduction Service No. ED320555).

Mani, G. (1988). Attitudes of external faculty towards distance education. In D. Stewart & J. Daniel (Eds.), *Developing distance education* (pp. 197–300), Oslo, Norway: International Council for Distance Education.

McNeil. D. (1990). Wiring the Ivory Tower: A round table on technology in higher education. Washington, D.C.: Academy for Education Development.

Okimoto, H. K., & Metcalf, S. I. (1991). Educational technology and you: Providing for faculty-learner support. *Proceedings from the Seventh Annual Conference on Distance Teaching and Learning* (pp. 220–224). Madison, WI: School of Education.

Ostendorf, V. A. (1994). The two-way video classroom. Littleton, CO: Author.

Parer, M. (1988). *Institutional support and rewards for academic staff involved in distance education.* Victoria, Australia: Center for Distance Learning, Gippsland Institute.

Pittman, S. W. (1994). *An exploratory study of the diffusion of instructional computing innovation among social work faculty.* Unpublished doctoral dissertation, University of Illinois at Urbana-Champaign.

Potts, M. K., & Hagan, C. B. (2000). Going the distance: Using systems theory to design, implement and evaluate a distance education program. *Journal of Social Work Education, 36*(1), 131–146.

Purdy, L., & Icenogle, D. (1976). *Classic theatre: The humanities in drama: Final research report.* Unpublished paper, Coastline Community College, Costa Mesa, CA.

Raymond, F. B. (1996). Delivering the MSW curriculum to non-traditional students through interactive television. In E. T. Reck (Ed.), *Modes of professional education II: The electronic social work curriculum in the twenty-first century. Tulane Studies in Social Welfare, 20.* New Orleans, LA: Tulane University.

Rogers, E. M. (1962). *Diffusion of innovations* (1st ed.). New York: Free Press.

Rogers, E. M. (1973). *Lessons from the diffusion of agricultural innovations.* Paper presented at the National Seminar on the Diffusion of New Instructional Materials and Practices, Racine, WI. (ERIC Document Reproduction Service No. ED083111).

Rogers, E. M. (1983). *Diffusion of innovations* (3rd ed.). New York: Free Press.

Rogers, E. M., Daley, H. M., & Wu. T. D. (1982). The diffusion of home computers: An exploratory study (Report No. IR101860). Palo Alto, CA: Stanford University, Institute for Communication Research. (ERIC Document Reproduction Service No. ED235786)

Rogers, E. M., & Jain, N. C. (1968). *Needed research on diffusion within educational organizations.* Paper presented at the National Conference on the Diffusion of Educational Ideas, East Lansing, MI (ERIC Document Reproduction Service No. ED017740)

Rogers, E. M. & Kincaid, D. L. (1981). *Communication networks.* New York: Free Press.

Rogers, E. M., Rogers, R. A., & Lee, C. C. (1975). *Diffusion of impact innovations to university professors.* Ann Arbor, MI: Michigan State University, Department of Journalism. (ERIC Document Reproduction Service No. ED 116 707).

Rogers, E. M., & Shoemaker, F. F. (1971). *Communication of innovation: A cross-cultural approach.* New York: Free Press.

Rompf, E. L. (1999). Program guidelines for long distance education initiatives: Overcoming faculty resistance. *Arete, 23*(1), 11–22.

Rothman, J. (1974). *Planning and organizing for social change: Action principles from social science research.* New York: Columbia University Press.

Schrock, S. A. (1985). Faculty perceptions of instructional development and the success/failure of an instructional development program: A naturalistic study. *Educational Communication and Technology Journal, 33,* 16–25.

Scriven, B. (1986). Staff attitudes to external studies. *Media in Education and Development, 19*(4), 176–183.

Seay, R., Rudolph, H. R., & Chamberlain, D. H. (2001). Faculty perceptions of interactive television. *Journal of Education for Business, 77*(i2), 99–106.

Siaciwena, R. (1989). Staff attitudes towards distance education in the University of Zambia. *Journal of Distance Education, 4*(2), 47–62.

Siegel, E., &.Jennings, J. G (1998). Distance learning in social work education: Results and Implications of a national survey. *Journal of Social Work Education, 34*(1), 71–81.

Smith, F. A. (1991). Interactive instructional strategies: Ways to enhance learning by television. *Proceedings from the Seventh Annual Conference on Distance Teaching and Learning* (pp. 125–128). Madison, WI: School of Education.

Tarde, G. (1903). *The laws of imitation.* (E. C. Parsons, Trans.). New York: Henry Holt.

Taylor, J., & White, V. (1991). Faculty attitudes towards teaching in the distance education mode: An exploratory investigation. *Research in Distance Education, 3*(3), 7–11.

Verduin J. R., & Clark, T. A. (1991). *Distance education: The foundations of effective practice.* San Francisco: Josey-Bass.

Walker, D. (1976). Toward comprehensions of curriculum realities. In L. Shulman (Ed.), *Review of research in education* (pp. 180–192). Chicago, IL: Peacock.

Walsh, S. M. (1993). *Attitudes and perceptions of university faculty toward technology based distance education.* Unpublished doctoral dissertation, University of Oklahoma. Norman.

Weinbach, R. W. (1985). *Evaluation of the interactive closed circuit television (ICCT) method.* Columbia: University of South Carolina, College of Social Work.

PART 5

The Future

Chapter 9

ISSUES AND THE FUTURE OF DISTANCE EDUCATION

Paul Abels

TERRA IGNOTA

Unsure of what lay beyond the explored world of Europe and the west coast of Africa, ancient map makers would often drew a vast ocean with huge waves and sea monsters, and in large italics might write *TERRA IGNOTA*—unknown territory. The drawings signified there were unknown dangers lurking out there. It was a warning to the voyager to be careful. Of course for a time there were those who believed that if you weren't careful and ventured into that vast unknown, you might fall off the end of the world, which at one time seemed more a certainty. These were well intended cautions and advice heeded by many. The certainty of falling off the end of the world proved wrong. Still, there are questions about those sea monsters. So with caution about drifting into the uncharted educational depths of distance education and social work, I will try to avoid those dreaded monsters and touch lightly on the possibilities of what lies "out there." What may you have to look forward to?

WILL YOU NEED TO BE CERTIFIED IN ORDER TO TEACH DISTANCE EDUCATION?

This is one of the strong possibilities evolving in DE's future. Currently a growing number of universities, including the University of Indiana, University of Illinois, University of Wisconsin, and California State University at Hayward among others, offer distance-education certification. A headline in the *Chronicle of Higher Education* reads, "Prospective distance educators flock to certification programs, but some academics question their value" (Carnevale, 2003, p. A31).

These programs range from a few courses and workshops to a masters' degree. "Penn State's certification program for distance education . . . consists of six courses. . . . The Penn Sate program is designed for people who want to run a distance-education program or be able to teach other instructors in distance learning" (p. A31.) Participants of the program often are seeking jobs or promotions; some are job hunting in business. At this time none of the institutions require faculty members be certified (p. A32). Is such training helpful? Certainly, but the question for us is, Is it necessary in the teaching of social work?

This is just one indicator of what the future holds for DE. Obviously, since universities are investing more in DE faculty training, they anticipate major growth in such programs. The American universities are also increasing their international exportation of DE programs, and other countries are increasing their own DE programs.

Is formal "training" of teachers valuable? Of course, yet it has not been a requirement in the social work profession. In interviewing prospective faculty for a position, whether or not they have had a course in pedagogy is never in question, nor does it appear with any frequency in their vitae.

If training for DE is important, should it not be just as important for all teachers at the university? In social work, few faculty have had a course in teaching. Many enter teaching directly from PhD programs, and their educational experience usually does not demonstrate a course in teaching. They learn on the job, and we see how the DE faculty learned from experience; none of the faculty had training in DE teaching. We can't know how they might have benefited, if at all, from such training. Be that as it may, there will be increased demand for such training; particularly as the use of communication technology in distance education and regular classroom settings expand.

There are those who forecast a "cyberspace classroom" with special attention paid to online education. As Palloff and Pratt (2001) state,

> Teaching in the cyberspace classroom requires that we mover beyond traditional models of pedagogy into new practices that are more facilitative. Teaching in cyberspace involves much more than simply taking old "tried and true" models of pedagogy and transferring them to a different medium. Unlike in the face-to-face classroom, in online distance education attention needs to be paid to developing a sense of community in the group of participants in order for the learning process to be successful. (p. 20)

Their discussion also addressed the kind of faculty who are suited to teach in DE, necessary training, and some of the tools required. The suitability of faculty is a factor, which will require quite extensive study, as we are still uncertain about some of the suitability requirements for teachers in general.

Building a Learning Community

The above statements related to the importance of building a sense of community is certainly reflected in the comments that a number of faculty and the liaison made in some of our previous chapters. It is also reflected in Palloff and Pratt's statement that

> The role of the group is critical to the success of the online class. A well-designed online class will intentionally build a learning community by providing opportunities for teamwork, the completion of collaborative assignments, and the ability to reflect on the process and the learning. Working with an online group can serve to reduce the sense of loneliness that some students have describes in taking on line classes that lack interaction. (p. 138)

The classroom becomes a temporary community; it is not made up of fleeting contacts, but a situation in which the students see each other for an entire day, once a week over a 3-year period. And as in many communities, norms of cooperation and trust need to develop if the communities are to develop their potential (Abels, 1977). The classroom, in a sense, is the workplace for many of the students, and as Bennis and Slater (1969) point out, the workplace becomes a temporary society. In becoming a temporary society, "there will be task forces composed of groups of relative strangers with diverse profes-sional backgrounds and skills organized around problems to be solved" (p. 98). The following excerpt by one of social work's premier educators illustrates the process of individuals evolving into a work-ing group and community of learners.

Bertha Reynolds, who later became a faculty member at Smith College, relates her experience as one of 25 students in a class for su-pervisors and teachers of social work given at Smith's College of So-cial Work. She describes some of their confusion, as experienced teachers themselves, about whether to be active or passive learners while taking a class given by the regular Smith faculty. As a group they worked on some of the problems they experienced.

> We had many problems to discuss about relationship to authority, for instance, the authority of position and that of expert knowledge and experience. We had to learn the right balance of listening and talking, of taking and giving out, in relationship to what was hap-pening in the lives of the people with whom we were working. (Reynolds, 1934, p. 200)
>
> Many of us got the subject of "relationship" in the learning-teaching process into our bones and sinew through the experience of swimming together . . . those who had not learned to swim be-cause of fear of the water were being taught by others. Several got the thrill of swimming alone for the first time. "I knew my teacher was right there and she would not let me drown." It was a relation-ship giving courage to try something new. (p. 202)

This real-life experience is a universal metaphor for how a group of individual students start to become a community.

> Many in the course gained new confidence in themselves through finding that, as a group working together, we could always be sure that something good would come out of this number of minds. "You can always trust a group" replaced the fear of frozen silence or of group domination with which most of us had come to experi-ence. To some of us, a group working together had meant fear of struggle for personal prestige, which we could now forget about as we took part in group thinking under good leadership. (p. 202)

Reynolds used these experiences reflectively and went on to write a fine book on teaching and learning (Reynolds, 1965).

In discussing the kind of collaborative learning in distance education that Reynolds talked about in her face-to-face experiences, Palloff and Pratt quote from an earlier work on the importance of collaborative learning:

> The learning process, then, involves self-reflection on the knowledge acquired about the course, about how learning occurs electronically, about the technology itself and about how the user has been transformed by their newfound relationships, with the machine, the software, the learning process and the other participants. (Palloff & Pratt, 1999, p. 62; Palloff & Pratt, 2001, p. 33)

Ethical Considerations in Distance Education

As distance education becomes a more commonly used tool in both academic and business circles, the importance of ethical considerations becomes paramount. We noted earlier the possible altering of interactive education to presentation of "canned" lectures as a cost-saving mechanism for educational institutions.

Access and the digital divide are a major problem, particularly in those universities serving large numbers of minority and economically disadvantaged students. Recalling some of the requirements that Buchanan noted in chapter 1, we know that affording computers and printers with the latest technologies has been out of reach for many. Van Dusen (2000) writes:

> Lack of Internet access results in information poverty for several classes of individuals and creates a new class of postsecondary institutions. An ever widening digital divide between the information haves and the have-nots exacerbates an already documented trend, first evident in the 1980's . . . toward greater income inequality in American Society (*The State of Working America*, 1960). (Van Dusen, p. 92)

The *digital divide*—an interesting concept, phrased in code words that cloak the seriousness of the problem, particularly at a time when funds for education have been drastically cut. It is not like the mountainous Great Divide that formed a barrier between the East and the West for those who sought the promise of rewards. The digital divide is a metaphor that reflects the fact that poor children cannot afford computers; that students in primarily segregated schools lack opportunities to learn to use the computer and the advanced educational and economic opportunities it provides. It also handicaps economically struggling universities, as well as the developing nations that do not have the technology to compete with technologically rich countries. The more technology advances and the higher the cost, the greater the loss to those trying to cross that great digital divide. Surely these are tasks for a profession dedicated to social justice to take on.

Some efforts are being initiated to remedy these concerns. For example *Better Opportunities Through Online Education* is a collaborative program between the University of Maryland college and local community organizations. The program provides computers, a printer, Internet access, and other materials, all without cost to students who could not otherwise afford them (Carlson, 2003). Still there are many low-income students unable to participate in programs such as this one. The lack of funds limits the number of students the college can accept, leading to a vigorous screening process that requires some knowledge of technology.

The federal government has tried to remedy some of the discrepancies in the digital divide and offered legislation to try to narrow that divide. A bill to provide technology grants to minority-serving institutions passed in the U.S. Senate this summer. The general thinking is that funding is inadequate considering the number of traditional minority serving institutions. Virginia Union, a historically black college (HBC), is one of the first HBCs to have a wireless Internet network, but only 15% of students own computers.

> More than two years ago Virginia Union considered requiring all students to have their own laptops. For now that idea has been abandoned. More than 90 percent of the college students receive financial aid. So asking them to spend more than $1000 each for a laptop would be too burdensome, says [the president of the college] Mr. Franlyn Foster. (Foster, 2003, p. A27)

In a study reported by Green and O'Brien (2000), the matter of the Internet digital divide was noted as a major concern. In reporting teacher responses the authors note, "Despite their efforts to level the playing field however, all teachers felt the student with Internet access have an advantage over those who did not." (p. 50). The problem is still unsolved, at least for the most disadvantaged.

Kanwar and Lentell (2002) note, "Education and training using the methods of distance education can be a profitable business delivered by global corporations or educational foundations with no requirements to address local or national needs. Education is a commodity to be traded on the world market" (p. 1).

As if saying "Amen" to that statement, Carnevale and Olsen (2003) write,

> Think of it as "the sweet spot." It's the segment of the American population coveted by the most successful online-education programs.
>
> It's working professionals who want to advance their careers by taking courses part time. It's executives who travel frequently but want to earn graduate degrees. It's parents who want to finish their undergraduate work without missing their kids' Saturday soccer games. (p. A31)

"Open learning as distance education is borderless in concept" (Blight, Davis, & Olsen, 1999, p. 16). It is difficult to imagine that the technology will not be used in ways that benefit certain countries or ideas. Certainly, economic rewards will also determine the extent to which DE can be instituted, particularly in developing nations.

Of course not all international organizations use DE as a trading commodity. Some are committed to distance education as a means of raising the social, economic, and educational levels of developing nations. One such international organization is the World Bank Group that has involved itself in a number of such activities:

1. **The World Links for Development** program which "links students and teachers in secondary schools in developing countries with students and teachers in industrialized countries for collaborative research, teaching and learning programs via the Internet"
2. **A Global Distance Education Net,** "a knowledge guide to distance education designed to help clients of the World Bank and others interested in using distance education for human development."
3. **Telecommunications and Informatics** is a site containing a "range of information and communications" (The World Bank Group, 2003)

In addition they are strongly committed to the concept of social capital and its relationship to information technology. They define social capital as "the institutions, relationships, and norms that shape the quality and quantity of a Society's social interactions" (The World Bank Group, 1999).

A recent study reported on in the *Chronicle of Higher Education* (Kiernon, 2003) reports that "distance education at American colleges expanded substantially the online-education takeoff of the late 1990s" (p. 28). Video conferencing was being used by 51% of the organizations. It is estimated that 2,876,000 students enrolled in distance education. The study by the U.S. Department of Education also reported that most colleges offering DE were larger institutions with students of 10,000 or more. "The divide is not surprising," said Jack M. Wilson, chief executive officer of UmassOnline. Private institutions tend to focus on offering residential students a high-quality experience," he said, "while public institutions are more concerned with offering reasonably priced education to the public, for which online education is well suited" (p. 28).

It appears that DE programs are now part of the class struggle; the elite smaller institutions seem to prefer not to be involved, suggesting that the education is not of "high quality." Once again the great divide enters the scene and may certainly influence the way distance education is perceived by various institutions.

"Many college administrators say the quality of their institutions' online courses may soon eclipse that of their brick-and-mortar offerings according to a report released this month, reports a survey conducted by Babson College and the Sloan consortium, an organization that promotes standards for online learning" (Chronicle, ONLINE, 2003, p. A30). Yet, some concerned with distance education do not share the optimistic conclusions suggested by that survey.

In their introduction to a collection of articles entitled *Distance Education: Issues and Concerns* (Maddux, Ewing-Taylor, & Johnson, 2002), with a much to be appreciated straightforwardness, state

> [I]t is with considerable ambivalence that we introduce the topic on distance education. The ambivalence is not because we doubt the potential of distance education to improve, or to revolutionize education. . . . Our ambivalence is because we think distance education, like every new technology, has both a light and dark side. . . . One of the most serious of these problems is a lack of attention to educational quality control issues." (pp. 1–2)

The authors go on to discuss the mushrooming of shoddy diploma mills and the various online degrees on all levels, but also note, "It is ironic that this and many of the of the other serious problems involving distance education are not technical in nature, but can be traced to a critical lack of principled leadership on campuses across the country" (p. 2). They recognize the commercialization of education and that much of what is occurring in distance education reflects changes in society. The series of articles in their issue cover those and other important issues.

CONCLUSION

No matter the economic accommodations, and the social class struggles that may be lying slightly underground, it is clear from all current reports that the future of distance education is ensured. Its continued growth in social work will only be limited if future research begins to illustrate a difference in the practice abilities of those in DE that do not measure up to the traditional classroom experience. It may very well be that the sense of community that a number of authors commented on will serve to enhance the ability of the DE graduate to incorporate the importance of community into their practice. Although some DE instructors try to include work with communities and groups, the educational experiences do not feature those aspects of social work practice as they have the teaching of individual counseling skills. This is partly true due to the trends in our profession but even more strongly exhibited in DE programs because of limited fieldwork opportunities in those areas. Even at a time of virtual universities (Carnevale, 2003), it is difficult to imagine virtual group or community organization experiences for students.

If one were to try to imagine where DE in social work will be in the next decade we might envision the students with their cell phones tuned into the class, because they were unable to make the distance leap or had to take care of their child. The classroom experience is still interactive and the students could see the other classes and communicate via the cell phone. Of course the research no doubt would show they are equally prepared and perhaps even more satisfied with the educational experience than those who travel to the classroom.

There is still the problem of the field experience, the one major educational requirement that differentiates social work DE from others. That experience has not kept up with technology changes, except perhaps for record keeping. How might we technologize the field experience? The answer, of course, is to create a virtual client system with which the student would interact. That is not too far off from the use of case material but could easily be translated into a computer game, in which the worker is faced with various problems a family, a community, or a school visit springs on him or her at a home visit or in the office. Their responses might instantaneously be assessed and commented on by the computer, with a "great" or an "ugh" or a question about why they did what they did, and even some alternatives. It would have to be approved by the CSWE, but in time as DE becomes more entrenched CSWE might be willing to allow an experimental virtual group for one semester. Chances are the results would indicate that their responses "passed" the judgments of those in a blind study who might assess those who deal with real clients and those who dealt with virtual clients.

If we have virtual universities, why not virtual agencies, clients, and communities? Many agencies have had to withdraw their staff from supervising students because of financial cuts and loss of staff. This has created problems for educators in finding and developing field placements, some are not up to desired standards, and some are serving more than they feel appropriate as an obligation to the profession. This may lead to less-than-the best educational experience. Perhaps during their last semester the students can have real-life experience, just to acclimate them to the real world.

The little trip into social science-fiction is based on technology that already exists and could be developed for social work if so desired. In 1971, in an article on the future, I suggested cloning Jane Addams; it seemed outlandish then, still is now, but not quite as much (Abels, 1971). I also anticipated the use of computers in social work, the concerns about control, and the digital divide (although that term was not generally in use at that time, if it existed at all). Those ideas turned out to be not so outlandish. For example, in what way does the material in the World Bank's DE program reflect its philosophy and shape the thinking of those using the program? How do the CSWE mandates for teaching generalist practice shape the thinking of students around community organization or work with groups, or the profession's more historic mission?

However, I never anticipated the Internet and the World Wide Web, which is the point I want to make here. We can't even imagine what new developments might take place in the next decade that would make our above scenario obsolete. What might the future bring? In addition to DE, there is counseling on the Web, and the cell phone makes it possible to do social work on the run, complete with visual interaction. Clients and workers need not be in the same place.

Marriage counseling could take place in triangulated conversations from three different points, or I could put a client on hold and get advice from my supervisor right on the spot, and so on. Will that increased development and use of technology help the profession accomplish its mission? Are we sure what DE is preparing all our students for?

Our profession will take advantage of the new technologies, and rightfully so. There may be differences among our social work educators and among our accrediting bodies about the direction to take. We have witnessed the acceptance of part time social work degree programs, the acceptance of the BA as the beginning professional degree, and the admission of private practitioners into NASW after a hard-fought resistance. We have seen the awarding of advanced credit for the master's program from one semester to 1 year and the acceptance of the distance education program. History suggests that as the social context and the technology changes, our profession will match the changes, and as our authors have shown, it will be done with skill and dedication. In a profession with a history such as ours, the voices they hear of their teachers and colleagues will not let them do otherwise.

REFERENCES

Abels, P. (1977). *The new practice of supervision and staff development.* New York: Associated Press.

Abels, P. (1973, 3 November). Will the real Jane Addams stand up? *Social Work, 18*(6), 36–39.

Bennis, W. G., & Slater, P. E. (1969). *The temporary society.* New York: Harper.

Blight, D., Davis, D., & Olsen, A. (1999). The internationalism of higher education. In Keith (Ed.), *Higher education through open and distance learning.* London: Routledge.

Carnevale, D. (2003). Learning online to teach online. *Chronicle of Higher Education, 50*(10), A30–32.

Carnevale, D., & Olsen, F. (2003). How to succeed in distance education. *Chronicle of Higher Education, 49,* A31–33.

Foster, A. L. (2003). Playing catch-up. *Chronicle of Higher Education, 49*(42), A27–28.

Green, D., & O'Brien, T (2002). The Internet's impact on the teacher, practice, and classroom culture. *The Journal: Technical Horizons Education, 20*(1), 44–51.

Kanwar, A., & Lentell, H. (2002). *Ethics in eistance education: Are we prepared to face the challenge?* Presented at workshop for the Pan-Commonwealth Forum on Open Learning. http:/www.col.org/pcf2/papers%5Ckanwar.pdf

Kiernan, V. (2003). A survey document: Growth in distance education in late 1990's. *Chronicle of Higher Education, 49*(45), A28.

Maddux, C. D., Ewing-Taylor, J., & Johnson. L. (2002). The light and dark sides of distance education. *Computers in the Schools, 19*(3/4), 1–9.

Palloff, R., & Pratt, K. (1999). *Building learning communities in cyberspace: Effective strategies for the online classroom.* San Francisco: Jossey-Bass.

Palloff, R., & Pratt, K. (2001). *Lessons from the cyberspace classroom.* San Francisco: Josey-Bass.

Read, B. (2003). Survey finds college administrators optimistic about future of online education. *The Chronicle Daily News//chronicle.com/pm/daily/ 2003/09/200309040/htm.* Retrieved Sept. 9, 2003.

Reynolds, B. (1934). *Between client and community.* New York: Oriole Editions.

Reynolds, B. (1965). *Learning and teaching in the practice of social work.* New York: Russell & Russell.

World Bank Group. (1999). *What is Social Capital?* Retrieved March, 2001. http://www.world bank.org/poverty/scapital/whatsc.htm.

World Bank Group. (2003). *Issues: Information and Communications.* http://worldbank.org/html/schools/issues/infocomm.htm.

Van Dusen, G. C. (2000). *Digital dilemma issues of access, cost and quality in media enhanced and distance education.* an Francisco: Jossey-Bass.

APPENDIX: ADDRESSING THE THESIS THROUGH DISTANCE EDUCATION

Thesis advisement at a distance involves both challenges and rewards. In my experience, the rewards are similar to those I've obtained through my relationships with on-campus students. Mentoring can occur. Both emotional and technical support can be provided. After the struggle of thesis conceptualization and implementation, when the final document has been submitted to the library, there is a similar level of gratification for a job well done and a similar number of thank-you cards and gifts from a grateful cohort. But there are special challenges due to the lack of ongoing face-to-face communication. I will first describe my program's thesis model, followed by techniques for minimizing these challenges.

THESIS MODEL

Our program's research sequence contains four required courses: computers (with emphasis on Internet communication and statistical analysis), research methods, and two semesters of thesis. In research methods, the primary assignment is to develop a preliminary thesis proposal. This provides a "head start" upon entering Thesis I. The proposal evolves over time, but few students change their topic entirely. They at least have a beginning literature review at this time. A thesis advisor is assigned at the beginning of Thesis I, along with two other committee members. Thesis I involves submission of a final proposal, a data gathering instrument, a protocol to the Institutional Review Board (IRB) for the Protection of Human Subjects (if applicable), and a draft literature review chapter. Thesis II involves data gathering and the remaining four chapters.

TECHNIQUES FOR MINIMIZING CHALLENGES

If possible, one person should be assigned as the single thesis advisor for a distance education site. This obviously facilitates travel when in-person visits are made. It also reduces confusion. Each thesis advisor has his or her own style and distance education cohorts tend to be extremely cohesive. They do talk with each other and compare notes. If I say one thing and another thesis advisor says something else, we both will be flooded with requests for clarification.

Holding a group orientation at the beginning of the thesis process is valuable if not essential. First, this is efficient because everyone has to receive the same information. Second, anxieties can be reduced as questions are addressed. The orientation can be done through interactive television, but an in-person visit at the beginning of the thesis process allows individual meetings to be held at the same time.

Individual meetings are important at the beginning of the process. Each student should have the opportunity to discuss his or her ideas thoroughly, and idiosyncratic issues need to be addressed. Often, a brainstorming dialogue is needed between the student and advisor. Is the sample really available? Will this study ever be approved by the IRB or is it too sensitive, intrusive, or risky? Is the preliminary proposal truly feasible, in reality, to implement in less than two semesters? What is the student's work style? How much structure does he or she need?

Handouts are essential. In addition to the usual Thesis Policy (or syllabus), one should provide a suggested calendar, with many interim deadlines, to maintain momentum. It is easy to lose track of on-campus students' progress and perhaps even easier to lose track of distance education students' progress. Because in-person communication will be limited, one should provide samples of IRB protocols and informed consent letters, along with a suggested outline for each chapter.

After the initial group orientation and individual meetings, the thesis advisor returns home and awaits the deluge of e-mailed proposals and instruments, followed by the deluge of e-mailed IRB protocols and consent letters. Students appreciate knowing that their work has been received. When I cannot review their materials quickly, I have found that a quick note back, acknowledging their existence and telling them that I'll respond in-depth within a few days or a even few weeks, is very reassuring.

At this time, track editing becomes a lifesaver. The "Track Changes" function of Microsoft Word allows one to delete words in one color, add words in another color, and insert all sorts of parenthetical comments. Students receive their work back as a track edited attachment. I suggest that they print out the edited document and work from their original document; another option of track editing is to accept or reject changes one by one.

Committee review of proposals (and the final thesis) can be handled in the same manner. IRB submission may require mailing hard copies of materials. As chapters are written, track editing continues. It is important to maintain contact with all students, especially those who are behind schedule based on the suggested calendar. Most of this can be done via e-mail, with telephone contact for special issues needing trouble-shooting (e.g., unclear or conflicting committee feedback, unclear IRB feedback, problems with data gathering, and overly anxious students in need of additional reassurance).

Another in-person visit should occur at the time of data analysis (unless an experienced local person is available to resolve the many problems that first-time SPSS users encounter). I have spent several marathon weekends in computer labs at distance education sites, reminding them how to enter data, watching as they run their analyses, and helping them interpret their output. We then block out tables for the Results chapter. It is also important to meet individually with students who are not conducting a quantitative study, in order to discuss the interpretation and presentation of their results.

The primary challenge here is that some students will have failed to gather their data on schedule due to unforeseen delays, tendencies to procrastinate, and life circumstances. However, one can at least help them set up their dataset, finalize an analysis strategy, and block out preliminary tables. Datasets and outputs can be e-mailed just as easily as text documents. And I have spent a few hours on the telephone, going step by step through each SPSS command, while they worked at their end, and then helping them understand their e-mailed output.

Final chapters are written, e-mailed, track edited, e-mailed back, rewritten, and submitted to committee for feedback. Library submission will undoubtedly require a hard copy, so mailing time needs to be considered. (In some rural communities, I have learned that "overnight" delivery takes several days.) Depending on institutional requirements regarding final thesis submission, staff support is probably essential—to deal with committee and dean/director signatures, to carry the final document to the library, to pick it up after it has been reviewed for formatting, to communicate format revisions, and to carry the final, final document to the library once more. Further complications needing staff support may include microfilm agreement forms, copyright forms, and procedures for paying binding and copying costs.

REWARDS

Thesis advisement from a distance, as with on-campus students, can seem overwhelming at times, but the rewards are great. In my experience, there are some special rewards unique to distance education. If the program is offered in a small rural community, the results may have a particularly significant impact. This is partially due to the fact that distance education students tend to be older and more experienced than on-campus students. In an environment where MSWs are scarce, they often hold high-level positions in agencies. Because their agencies are smaller, most have ready access to administrators. A few actually *are* the administrators. As such, they have the power to implement their findings. The ubiquitous "implications for social work practice and/or policy" section of the thesis is more likely to become a reality. This is analogous to the "big fish, little pond" phenomenon. Although urban MSW students may be small- or medium-size fish in a large pond (i.e., bureaucracy), rural MSW students tend to be big fish in a little pond. They may serve on school boards, be members of boards of directors, hold political office, socialize with county commissioners, and be close friends of the mayor. In addition, because distance education theses are likely to be *about* the local community, they are likely to be *read* by the local community, particularly when the agency setting is easily identifiable. I have never known an on-campus student who was required to sign an agreement prohibiting release of a thesis to the press before the agency had a chance to review the findings. This has occurred several times among my distance education thesis students.

Finally, having recently returned from one of our distance education site's graduation ceremonies, I must emphasize the most profound rewards of all—sharing their relief at finishing their thesis, revisiting their initial disbelief that they were capable of such a feat, and witnessing their pride in their accomplishment.

INDEX

Springer Publishing Company

Successful Grant Writing
Strategies for Health and Human Service Professionals, Second Edition

Laura N. Gitlin, PhD and Kevin J. Lyons, PhD

Designed for health and human service professionals in academic and practice settings, this book will assist inexperienced grant writers as well as those who have had success but would like to expand their knowledge of grantmanship. The authors provide a framework for understanding the funding world and offer a range of effective strategies and work models for success in obtaining external support. The appendices contain a selection of common questions and their answers and a list of key acronyms.

SUCCESSFUL
GRANT
WRITING
*Strategies for Health and
Human Service Professionals*
Second Edition

LAURA N. GITLIN
KEVIN J. LYONS

SPRINGER PUBLISHING COMPANY

Second Edition Topics include:

- A Research Career Trajectory
- Pilot Research Programs
- What Ideas are Hot and What are Not
- The NIH Modular Format
- Elements of a Concept Paper
- Managing the Grant Award

Partial Contents:

Part I: The Perspective of the Funding Agencies • Getting Started • Becoming Familiar with Funding Sources

Part II: The Perspective of the Grantee • Developing Your Ideas for Funding • Learning About Your Institution

Part III: Writing the Proposal • Common Sections of Proposals • Preparing a Budget • Technical Considerations • Strategies for Effective Writing

Part IV: Models for Proposal Development • Four Project Structures • The Process of Collaboration

Part V: Life After a Proposal Submission • Understanding the Review Process • A Case Study

Part VI: Receiving the Grant Award • Managing the Grant Award

2004   320pp   0-8261-9261-0   soft

11 West 42nd Street, New York, NY 10036-8002 • **Fax: 212-941-7842**
Order Toll-Free: 877-687-7476 • **Order On-line: www.springerpub.com**